I0157214

PETALS AT YOUR FEET

PETALS AT YOUR FEET

Atma Bodha and Selected Devotionals

Swamini Sri Lalitambika Devi

MAHAKAILASA ASHRAM
New York, New York

© 2016 Chintamani Books
Mahakailasa Ashram
New York, New York
All rights reserved.
ISBN 978-0-9960236-3-4

CONTENTS

DEDICATION

THE LORD IS KNOWN *through various names and forms and graces the seeker with myriad and infinite blessings. So, the Lord is worshiped. Beyond the romance of devotional ritual, however, with its lamps, incense, petals, sweets, and love songs, all is one.*

May we honor all forms of the Lord in each religion, as well as no name or form at all.

May we bow down to each being as an expression of transcendent truth.

In this way, we awaken.

Spiritual awakening brings peace to all. May we respect the earth, the waters, the fire, the sky, and the infinite space; and may we love all beings as our relations. May we share of our resources, so that the children grow up with enough to eat and access to education. May we live without the threat of violence. May we serve with compassion, everywhere.

This book was compiled as an offering for Sivaratri 2016. May all beings be liberated.

DEVOTIONAL
HYMNS

॥ गनेश पन्चरत्नम् ॥

मुदाकरात्तमोदकं सदा विमुक्तिसाधकं
कलाधरावतंसकं विलासिलोकरक्षकम् ।
अनायकैकनायकं विनाशितेभदैत्यकं
नताशुभाशुनाशकं नमामि तं विनायकम् ॥ १ ॥

नतेतराति भीकरं नवोदितार्क भास्वरं
नमत्सुरारिनिर्जरं नताधिकापदुद्धरम् ।
सुरेश्वरं निधीश्वरं गजेश्वरं गणेश्वरं
महेश्वरं तमाश्रयं परात्परं निरन्तरम् ॥ २ ॥

समस्तलोकशंकरं निरस्तदैत्यकुञ्जरं
दरेतरोदरं वरं वरेभवक्त्रमक्षरम् ।
कृपाकरं क्षमाकरं मुदाकरं यशस्करं
मनस्करं नमस्कृतां नमस्करोमि भास्वरम् ॥ ३ ॥

अकिंचनार्तिमार्जनं चिरन्तनोक्तिभाजनं
पुरारिपूर्वनन्दनं सुरारिगर्वचर्वणम् ।
प्रपञ्चनाशभीषणं धनंजयादिभूषणम्
कपोलदानवारणं भजे पुराणवारणम् ॥ ४ ॥

नितान्तकान्तदन्तकान्तिमन्तकान्तकात्मजं
अचिन्त्यरूपमन्तहीनमन्तरायकृन्तनम् ।
हृदन्तरे निरन्तरं वसन्तमेव योगिनां
तमेकदन्तमेव तं विचिन्तयामि सन्ततम् ॥ ५ ॥

महागणेशपञ्चरत्नमादरेण योऽन्वहं
प्रजल्पति प्रभातके हृदि स्मरन् गणेश्वरम् ।
अरोगतामदोषतां सुसाहितीं सुपुत्रतां
समाहितायुरष्टभूतिमभ्युपैति सोऽचिरात् ॥ ६ ॥

GANESA PANCHARATNAM

I bow to Lord Vinayaka,
  who offers joy in hand like a sweet,
  who strives ever for the true
  seeker's liberation.
Adorned with the moon,
  he is happy to protect creation.
He is master to himself,
  as he is to the seeker,
  and vanquishes the inner demons.
If you surrender to him, he will rapidly
  destroy whatever is not blessed for you.
I bow and surrender to Lord Vinayaka.   1

I bow to Lord Vinayaka
  who frightens the arrogant enemy.
For the true seeker, his benevolence
  rises like the dawn.
He is ever vital and will never perish.
The shining ones revere him as their Lord.
He is the Lord of light and abundance,
  he of elephant head whom the celestials adore.
Surrender, and he will carry you through all troubles.
He is mighty, greater than anything in this world,
  and I take refuge in him.
I surrender to him, evermore.   2

I bow to Lord Vinayaka,
  who enlivens all aspects of creation
  and tramples every obstacle.
Of ample form, he embodies prosperity
  and boons with abundant blessing.
His radiant face reflects
  the imperishable light within.
He showers grace, forgiveness, joy,
  and glory upon the true seeker.
He blesses the reverent with intelligence
  and clear understanding.
I bow to the light of his form.   3

I bow to Lord Vinayaka,
  who obliterates all sorrows of the poor,
  who is a vessel rich with wisdom,
  who is son of the fabled demon-slayer,
  who bites the heads off of arrogance and pride,
  whose strength annihilates delusion,
  who clears the mind of desire.
Earth, water, fire, air, and space are his raiment.
From him flows the nectar of adoration,
  the blessings foretold by the sages.
I bow to the Lord.   4

I bow to Lord Vinayaka,
    whose one-tusked face is beautiful,
    whose form exceeds earthly bounds,
    who transcends concept and creation,
    who is born of the light beyond death.
I bow to the Lord who crushes all obstacles
    to awakening.
He dwells in the heart-cave of the *yogi*,
    so I meditate upon the Lord of one tusk.   5

Whosoever holds in mind with devotion
    these five jewels that praise Lord Ganesa
    and says this prayer at dawn,
    meditating upon Lord Ganesa,
    will be liberated from sin and illness,
    will know both strength and health.
The devout seeker will find true companions
    and will enjoy a long life.
The Lord will bestow eight great blessings—
    health, strength, contentment, abundance,
    power, wealth, success, and good fortune.
The seeker will be liberated.   6

—Sri Sankaracarya

॥ भज गोविन्दं ॥

भज गोविन्दं भज गोविन्दं
गोविन्दं भज मूढमते ।
संप्राप्ते सन्निहिते काले
नहि नहि रक्षति डुकिञ्करणे ॥ १ ॥

मूढ जहीहि धनागमतृष्णां
कुरु सद्बुद्धिम् मनसि वितृष्णाम् ।
यल्लभसे निज कर्मोपात्तं
वित्तं तेन विनोदय चित्तम् ॥ २ ॥

नारी स्तनभर नाभीदेशं
दृष्ट्वा मा गा मोहावेशम् ।
एतन्मांस वसादि विकारं
मनसि विचिन्तय वारं वारम् ॥ ३ ॥

नलिनी दलगत जलमति तरलं
तद्वज्जीवित मतिशय चपलम् ।
विद्धि व्याध्यभिमान ग्रस्तं
लोकं शोकहतं च समस्तम् ॥ ४ ॥

16

यावद्वित्तोपार्जन सक्तः
तावन्निजपरिवरो रक्तः ।
पश्चाज्जीवति जर्जर देहे
वार्तां कोऽपि न पृच्छति गेहे ॥५॥

यावत्पवनो निवसति देहे
तावत्पृच्छति कुशलं गेहे।
गतवति वायौ देहापाये
भार्या बिभ्यति तस्मिन्काये ॥६॥

बाल स्तावत्क्रीडासक्तः
तरुण स्तावत्तरुणीसक्तः ।
वृद्ध स्तावच्चिन्तासक्तः
परमे ब्रह्मणि कोऽपि न सक्तः ॥७॥

का ते कान्ता कस्ते पुत्रः
संसारोऽयमतीव विचित्रः ।
कस्य त्वं कः कुत आयातः
तत्त्वं चिन्तय तदिह भ्रातः ॥८॥

सत्सङ्गत्वे निस्सङ्गत्वं
निःसङ्गत्वे निर्मोहत्वम् ।
निर्मोहत्वे निश्चलतत्त्वं
निश्चलतत्त्वे जीवन्मुक्तिः ॥९॥

वयसि गते कः कामविकारः
शुष्के नीरे कः कासारः ।
क्षीणे वित्ते कः परिवारः
ज्ञाते तत्त्वे कः संसारः ॥१०॥

मा कुरु धनजन यौवन गर्वं
हरति निमेषात्कालः सर्वम् ।
मायामयमिदमखिलं बुद्ध्वा
ब्रह्मपदं त्वं प्रविश विदित्वा ॥११॥

दिन यामिन्यौ सायं प्रातः
शिशिर वसन्तौ पुनरायातः ।
कालः क्रीडति गच्छत्यायुः
तदपि न मुञ्चत्याशावायुः ॥१२॥

का ते कान्ता धन गत चिन्ता

वातुल किं तव नास्ति नियन्ता ।

त्रिजगति सज्जन सङ्गतिरेका

भवति भवार्णव तरणे नौका ॥ १३ ॥

जटिलो मुण्डी लुञ्जित केशः

काषायम्बर बहुकृत वेषः ।

पश्यन्नपि च न पश्यति मूढः

उदर निमित्तं बहुकृत वेषः ॥ १४ ॥

अङ्गं गलितं पलितं मुण्डं

दशन विहीनं जातं तुण्डम् ।

वृद्धो याति गृहीत्वा दण्डं

तदपि न मुञ्चत्याशापिण्डम् ॥ १५ ॥

अग्रे वह्निः पृष्ठे भानुः

रात्रौ चुबुक समर्पित जानुः ।

करतल भिक्षस्तरुतल वासः

तदपि न मुञ्चत्याशा पाशः ॥ १६ ॥

कुरुते गङ्गा सागर गमनं

व्रत परिपालनमथवा दानम् ।

ज्ञान विहीनः सर्वमतेन

भजति न मुक्तिं जन्म शतेन ॥ १७॥

सुरमन्दिर तरु मूल निवासः

शय्या भूतलमजिनं वासः ।

सर्व परिग्रह भोगत्यागः

कस्य सुखं न करोति विरागः ॥ १८॥

योगरतो वा भोगरतो वा

सङ्गरतो वा सङ्गविहीनः ।

यस्य ब्रह्मणि रमते चित्तं

नन्दति नन्दति नन्दत्येव ॥ १९॥

भगवद्गीता किञ्चिदधीता

गङ्गा जललव कणिका पीता ।

सकृदपि येन मुरारि समर्चा

क्रियते तस्य यमेन न चर्चा ॥ २०॥

पुनरपि जननं पुनरपि मरणं
पुनरपि जननी जठरे शयनम् ।
इह संसारे बहु दुस्तारे
कृपायाऽपारे पाहि मुरारे ॥ २१ ॥

रथ्या चर्पट विरचित कन्थः
पुण्यापुण्य विवर्जित पन्थः ।
योगी योग नियोजित चित्तः
रमते बालोन्मत्तवदेव ॥ २२ ॥

कस्त्वं कोऽहं कुत आयातः
का मे जननी को मे तातः ।
इति परिभावय सर्वमसारं
विश्वं त्यक्त्वा स्वप्नविचारम् ॥ २३ ॥

त्वयि मयि चान्यत्रैको विष्णुः
व्यर्थं कुप्यसि मय्यसहिष्णुः ।
भव समचित्तः सर्वत्र त्वं
वाञ्छस्यचिराद्यदि विष्णुत्वम् ॥ २४ ॥

शत्रौ मित्रे पुत्रे बन्धौ

मा कुरु यत्नं विग्रह सन्धौ ।

सर्वस्मिन्नपि पश्यात्मानं

सर्वत्रोत्सृज भेदाज्ञानम् ॥ २५ ॥

कामं क्रोधं लोभं मोहं

त्यक्त्वाऽऽत्मानं पश्यति सोऽहम् ।

आत्मज्ञान विहीना मूढाः

ते पच्यन्ते नरक निगूढाः ॥ २६ ॥

गेयं गीता नाम सहस्रं

ध्येयं श्रीपति रूपमजस्रम् ।

नेयं सज्जन सङ्गे चित्तं

देयं दीनजनाय च वित्तम् ॥ २७ ॥

सुखतः क्रियते रामाभोगः

पश्चाद्धन्त शरीरे रोगः ।

यद्यपि लोके मरणं शरणं

तदपि न मुञ्चति पापाचरणम् ॥ २८ ॥

अर्थमनर्थं भावय नित्यं

नास्ति ततः सुख लेशः सत्यम् ।

पुत्रादपि धनभाजां भीतिः

सर्वत्रैषा विहिता रीतिः ॥ २९ ॥

प्राणायामं प्रत्याहारं

नित्यानित्य विवेक विचारम् ।

जाप्यसमेत समाधि विधानं

कुर्वे वधानं महदवधानम् ॥ ३० ॥

गुरु चरणाम्बुज निर्भरभक्तः

संसारादचिराद्भव मुक्तः ।

सेन्दिय मानस नियमादेवं

द्रक्ष्यसि निज हृदयस्थं देवम् ॥ ३१ ॥

BHAJA GOVINDAM

Love the Lord, love the Lord. The Lord—
love him, bewildered one. You of foolish resolve,
memorizing and reciting grammatical rules
will not ward off death. When the time comes,
rote discipline cannot free you.   1

You who have gone astray, give up
    dogged repetition.
Let the thirst for wealth and pleasure
    be slaked like this:
Contemplate your deeds.
Accept what is now.
Devote yourself completely
    to knowing the Lord.   2

Love the Lord, love the Lord. The Lord—
love him, bewildered one. You of foolish resolve,
memorizing and reciting grammatical rules
will not ward off death. When the time comes,
rote discipline cannot free you.

Entranced by worldly love,
    stand strong. Attraction
    to flesh is delusion.
Resist rising desire.
Choose to know the Lord alone.   3

Love the Lord, love the Lord. The Lord—
love him, bewildered one. You of foolish resolve,
memorizing and reciting grammatical rules
will not ward off death. When the time comes,
rote discipline cannot free you.

A water droplet trembles
   against the lotus petal.
So, too, the soul bound
   by desire, pride, and sorrow
   may be unsure in this world.
Stay even-minded.   4

Love the Lord, love the Lord. The Lord—
love him, bewildered one. You of foolish resolve,
memorizing and reciting grammatical rules
will not ward off death. When the time comes,
rote discipline cannot free you.

While your youthful hands hold riches,
   loved ones will stay true;
   but no one in the house cares to speak
   to one who is old and feeble—
   forgotten.   5

Love the Lord, love the Lord. The Lord—
love him, bewildered one. You of foolish resolve,
memorizing and reciting grammatical rules
will not ward off death. When the time comes,
rote discipline cannot free you.

While the breath resides in your body,
   the family kindly inquires, caring
   for you; but when the breath departs,
   even those you hold most dear
   will abandon the corpse.   6

Love the Lord, love the Lord. The Lord—
love him, bewildered one. You of foolish resolve,
memorizing and reciting grammatical rules
will not ward off death. When the time comes,
rote discipline cannot free you.

A child plays.
Youth clings to beauty.
The responsible adult
   gets lost in worry.
When are we ever so
   absorbed in the Lord?   7

Love the Lord, love the Lord. The Lord—
love him, bewildered one. You of foolish resolve,
memorizing and reciting grammatical rules
will not ward off death. When the time comes,
rote discipline cannot free you.

Contemplate—Who truly is
   your most beloved,
   and who is your child?
Family bonds are bewildering.
After all, to whom do you belong,
   and from where did you come?
Ponder this deeply, now,
   for you are my kin.   8

Love the Lord, love the Lord. The Lord—
love him, bewildered one. You of foolish resolve,
memorizing and reciting grammatical rules
will not ward off death. When the time comes,
rote discipline cannot free you.

Keep company with the wise,
   and release passing attachments.
Renounce temporal pleasure
   and pain, and awaken
   from this world's delusion.
So, the mind steadies.
With mind absorbed in the Lord,
   the soul is liberated.   9

Love the Lord, love the Lord. The Lord—
love him, bewildered one. You of foolish resolve,
memorizing and reciting grammatical rules
will not ward off death. When the time comes,
rote discipline cannot free you.

When the vigor of youth is
   drained, who feels lust?
As the lake bed dries to desert,
   where go the playful waters?
With all wealth spent,
   can loved ones be sated?
When the knower goes
   beyond all this, who is left
   to experience sorrow?   10

Love the Lord, love the Lord. The Lord—
love him, bewildered one. You of foolish resolve,
memorizing and reciting grammatical rules
will not ward off death. When the time comes,
rote discipline cannot free you.

Do not crow of youth, wealth, or following.
Time steals all this in an instant.
Abandon illusion.
Give yourself over to
   knowing the Lord.   11

Love the Lord, love the Lord. The Lord—
love him, bewildered one. You of foolish resolve,
memorizing and reciting grammatical rules
will not ward off death. When the time comes,
rote discipline cannot free you.

Day and night,
   dawn and dusk,
     spring and winter
     revolve.
Time is amused,
   as life ebbs away.
Still, the bonds of desire
   do not slacken.   12

Love the Lord, love the Lord. The Lord—
love him, bewildered one. You of foolish resolve,
memorizing and reciting grammatical rules
will not ward off death. When the time comes,
rote discipline cannot free you.

So the one you desire, your most
cherished treasure, is gone.
Crazy fool, why worry?
Is all not given you to be renounced?
Nothing in the three worlds matters,
   except truth. Seek the company
   of fervent seekers and illumined sages.
Their wisdom is the raft that will
   carry you across the river of sorrows.   13

Love the Lord, love the Lord. The Lord—
love him, bewildered one. You of foolish resolve,
memorizing and reciting grammatical rules
will not ward off death. When the time comes,
rote discipline cannot free you.

Ascetics may be of shaven head
   or matted lock, and adorned
   with ochre robe.
Even so, they do not see
   what is real.
They are as foolish as any.
Their dress is a costume.   14

Love the Lord, love the Lord. The Lord—
love him, bewildered one. You of foolish resolve,
memorizing and reciting grammatical rules
will not ward off death. When the time comes,
rote discipline cannot free you.

Of weak limb, bald head, and toothless gum,
   an old man holds only to his staff.
Even so, the grip of desire does not slacken.   15

Love the Lord, love the Lord. The Lord—
love him, bewildered one. You of foolish resolve,
memorizing and reciting grammatical rules
will not ward off death. When the time comes,
rote discipline cannot free you.

Homeless, with the sun behind him
   and only a fire's comfort at night,
   the seeker curls chin to knees.
This beggar of open palm
   takes shelter beneath a tree.
Even so, the grip of desire does not slacken.   16

Love the Lord, love the Lord. The Lord—
love him, bewildered one. You of foolish resolve,
memorizing and reciting grammatical rules
will not ward off death. When the time comes,
rote discipline cannot free you.

A seeker who makes pilgrimage
   to the holy Ganges
   where the river meets the sea,
   who upholds vows and gives alms
   may yet lack heart.
No one will be liberated without devotion,
   though born a hundred times over.   17

Love the Lord, love the Lord. The Lord—
love him, bewildered one. You of foolish resolve,
memorizing and reciting grammatical rules
will not ward off death. When the time comes,
rote discipline cannot free you.

Dwelling in a temple or beneath a tree
  is all the same to one who has
  renounced possession and pleasure,
  and wrapped in deerskin,
  sleeps on the lap of the earth.
Who wouldn't be joyful
  having realized such dispassion?   18

Love the Lord, love the Lord. The Lord—
love him, bewildered one. You of foolish resolve,
memorizing and reciting grammatical rules
will not ward off death. When the time comes,
rote discipline cannot free you.

The seeker may yet desire
  austerity or pleasure,
  company or solitude;
  but one who delights in knowing the Lord
  rejoices, rejoices and is ever joyful.   19

Love the Lord, love the Lord. The Lord—
love him, bewildered one. You of foolish resolve,
memorizing and reciting grammatical rules
will not ward off death. When the time comes,
rote discipline cannot free you.

Let the seeker contemplate
  a single verse of the *Bhagavad Gita*,
  sip but a drop of Ganges water;
for one who abounds in
  the play of the Lord,
  one who worships like this,
  does not quarrel with death.   20

Love the Lord, love the Lord. The Lord—
love him, bewildered one. You of foolish resolve,
memorizing and reciting grammatical rules
will not ward off death. When the time comes,
rote discipline cannot free you.

Again and again, we are born to die;
for we seek the womb's comfort.
Here and everywhere, how difficult
   to break free from the revolution
   of birth and death.
Lord, in your grace, carry me.   21

Love the Lord, love the Lord. The Lord—
love him, bewildered one. You of foolish resolve,
memorizing and reciting grammatical rules
will not ward off death. When the time comes,
rote discipline cannot free you.

The seeker who roams in rags
   and follows the sun
     knows neither vice nor virtue.
Such a one lives with no companion
   but ecstasy.
Such a one may appear
   as a drunkard, a madman, or a child.   22

Love the Lord, love the Lord. The Lord—
love him, bewildered one. You of foolish resolve,
memorizing and reciting grammatical rules
will not ward off death. When the time comes,
rote discipline cannot free you.

Who are you? Who am I?
Who are you? Who am I?
Where did you come from?
Who are my mother and father?
One must inquire so
   to see through worldly delusion,
   as if waking from a dream.   23

Love the Lord, love the Lord. The Lord—
love him, bewildered one. You of foolish resolve,
memorizing and reciting grammatical rules
will not ward off death. When the time comes,
rote discipline cannot free you.

The Lord is in you, and the Lord is in me,
   for the Lord is everywhere.
Seeker of little patience—
   excitement and anger get you nowhere.
Be ever even-tempered,
   if you wish to know the Lord.   24

Love the Lord, love the Lord. The Lord—
love him, bewildered one. You of foolish resolve,
memorizing and reciting grammatical rules
will not ward off death. When the time comes,
rote discipline cannot free you.

Do not try to discern friend from foe.
Do not cling to worldly relations, at all.
Realize the Lord as the one in all.   25

Love the Lord, love the Lord. The Lord—
love him, bewildered one. You of foolish resolve,
memorizing and reciting grammatical rules
will not ward off death. When the time comes,
rote discipline cannot free you.

One who abandons worldly delusion,
   the lust, the fury, and the greed,
   realizes truth in all.
Inquire now into your real nature,
   for one without direct experience
   lives ever in quiet torment.   26

Love the Lord, love the Lord. The Lord—
love him, bewildered one. You of foolish resolve,
memorizing and reciting grammatical rules
will not ward off death. When the time comes,
rote discipline cannot free you.

Sing a song of praise.
Chant the thousand names.
Meditate upon the blessed
   form of the Lord.
Let the wise lead you.
Give to the miserable,
   downtrodden, and afflicted
   the wealth of truth.   27

Love the Lord, love the Lord. The Lord—
love him, bewildered one. You of foolish resolve,
memorizing and reciting grammatical rules
will not ward off death. When the time comes,
rote discipline cannot free you.

One who seeks happiness in
   the charms of carnal pleasure
   will know the shadow of malady.
Death is all this world can promise.
Even so, the crazy fool does not
   turn from vice.   28

Love the Lord, love the Lord. The Lord—
love him, bewildered one. You of foolish resolve,
memorizing and reciting grammatical rules
will not ward off death. When the time comes,
rote discipline cannot free you.

Money is finite and so worth little.
Possessions cannot hint
   at eternal fulfillment. What's more,
   the rich fear cunning offspring.
Such is the way of the world.   29

Love the Lord, love the Lord. The Lord—
love him, bewildered one. You of foolish resolve,
memorizing and reciting grammatical rules
will not ward off death. When the time comes,
rote discipline cannot free you.

Harness the life force,
   and rein in your attention.
Look within. Discern
   what is real from what is not.
Seek the absolute truth.
Chant, pray, meditate, and merge.
Do this with care.
Do this with great care.   30

Love the Lord, love the Lord. The Lord—
love him, bewildered one. You of foolish resolve,
memorizing and reciting grammatical rules
will not ward off death. When the time comes,
rote discipline cannot free you.

Ardent seeker, take refuge from
   the endless sorrow of this world
   in the lotus feet of the *guru.*
Soon, you will be free.
Master the mind. You will
   realize the Lord,
   who lives ever in the heart.   31

Love the Lord, love the Lord. The Lord—
love him, bewildered one. You of foolish resolve,
memorizing and reciting grammatical rules
will not ward off death. When the time comes,
rote discipline cannot free you.

—Sri Sankaracarya

NOTES

Verses 1-13 are attributed to Sri Sankaracarya, as are the
concluding verses 28-31. Verses 14-27 are said to have been
composed by the fourteen disciples who were with him that day
in Kasi.

   It is said that the group came upon an aging *pandit* who
was doggedly repeating grammatical rules for the sake of mere
intellectual accomplishment. So, Sri Sankaracarya and his
disciples began to sing the glories of devotion to the Lord, *Bhaja*
Govindam.

   These verses are also known as *Moha Mudgara.* This
title compares the hymn to a hammer that, with its ringing
refrain, shatters delusion.

॥ गोपी गीत ॥

जयति तेऽधिकं जन्मना व्रजः श्रयत इन्दिरा शश्वदत्र हि ।
दयित दृश्यतां दिक्षु तावकास्त्वयि धृतासवस्त्वां विचिन्वते ॥ १ ॥

शरदुदाशये साधुजातसत्सरसिजोदरश्रीमुषा दृशा ।
सुरतनाथ तेऽशुल्कदासिका वरद निघ्नतो नेह किं वधः ॥ २ ॥

विषजलाप्ययाद् व्यालराक्षसाद् वर्षमारुताद् वैद्युतानलात् ।
वृषमयात्मजाद् विश्वतोभयाद्‌ऋषभ ते वयं रक्षिता मुहुः ॥ ३ ॥

न खलु गोपिकानन्दनो भवानखिलदेहिनामन्तरात्मदृक् ।
विखनसार्थितो विश्वगुप्तये सख उदेयिवान् सात्वतां कुले ॥ ४ ॥

विरचिताभयं वृष्णिधुर्य ते चरणमीयुषां संसृतेर्भयात् ।
करसरोरुहं कान्त कामदं शिरसि धेहि नः श्रीकरग्रहम् ॥ ५ ॥

व्रजजनार्तिहन् वीर योषितां निजजनस्मयध्वंसनस्मित ।
भज सखे भवत्किङ्करीः स्म नो जलरुहाननं चारु दर्शय ॥ ६ ॥

प्रणतदेहिनां पापकर्शनं तृणचरानुगं श्रीनिकेतनम् ।
फणिफणार्पितं ते पदाम्बुजं कृणु कुचेषु नः कृन्धि हृच्छयम् ॥ ७ ॥

मधुरया गिरा वल्गुवाक्यया बुधमनोज्ञया पुष्करेक्षण ।
विधिकरीरिमा वीर मुह्यतीरधरसीधुनाऽप्याययस्व नः ॥८॥

तव कथामृतं तप्तजीवनं कविभिरीडितं कल्मषापहम् ।
श्रवणमङ्गलम् श्रीमदाततं भुवि गृणन्ति ते भूरिदा जना ॥९॥

प्रहसितं प्रिय प्रेमवीक्षण विहरण च ते ध्यानमङ्गलम् ।
रहसि संविदो या हृदिस्पृश कुहक नो मन क्षोभयन्ति हि ॥१०॥

चलसि यद् व्रजाच्चारयन् पशून् नलिनसुन्दर नाथ ते पदम् ।
शिलतृणाङ्कुरै सीदतीति न कलिलतां मन कान्त गच्छति ॥११॥

दिनपरिक्षये नीलकुन्तलैर्वनरुहाननं बिभ्रदावृतम् ।
घनरजस्वलं दर्शयन् मुहुर्मनसि न स्मर वीर यच्छसि ॥१२॥

प्रणतकामद पद्मजार्चितं धरणिमन्डनं ध्येयमापदि ।
चरणपङ्कजं शन्तमं च ते रमण नः स्तनेष्वर्पयाधिहन् ॥१३॥

सुरतवर्धनं शोकनाशन स्वरितवेणुना सुष्ठु चुम्बितम् ।
इतररागविस्मारणं नृणां वितर वीर नस्तेऽधरामृतम् ॥१४॥

अटति यद् भवानह्नि काननं त्रुटिर्युगायते त्वामपश्यताम् ।
कुटिलकुन्तलं श्रीमुखं च ते जड उदीक्षतां पक्ष्मकृद् दृशाम् ॥१५॥

पतिसुतान्वय भ्रातृबान्धवानतिविलङ्घ्य तेऽन्त्यच्युतागताः ।
गतिविदस्तवोद् गीतमोहिताः कितव योषितः कस्यजेन्निशि ॥ १६ ॥

रहसि संविदं हृच्छयोदयं प्रहसितांननं प्रेमवीक्षणम् ।
बृहदुरः श्रियो वीक्ष्य धाम ते मुहुरतिस्पृहा मुह्यते मनः ॥ १७ ॥

व्रजवनौ कसां व्यक्तिरङ्ग ते वृजिनहन्त्यलं विश्वमङ्गलम् ।
त्यज मनाक् च नस्त्वत्स्पृहात्मनां स्वजनहृद्रुजां यन्निषूदनम् ॥ १८ ॥

यत्ते सुजातचरणाम्बुरुहं स्तनेषु भीताः शनैः प्रिय दधीमहि कर्कशेषु ।
तेनाटवीमटसि तद् व्यथते न किंस्वित् कूर्पादिभिर्भ्रमति धीर्भवदायुषां नः ॥ १९ ।

GOPI GITA

Victory to your birth,
   to you who blessed this land.
Good fortune reigns here, now.
The cowherds rejoice in abundance,
   but we milkmaids weep,
   searching the forests for you.
Have mercy, and show yourself.   1

Your eyes are lotus flowers
   that bloom from spring waters.
Your glance conquers the heart.
We are your simple servants,
   so this longing for you feels like dying.
Lord, show yourself.   2

From the serpent, from the rain—
   you saved us.
From wind, fire, and wicked disaster—
   you saved us.
Why let us die now?   3

You are not a cowherd's son. You
   are the soul, the breath of creation,
   born as a village lad to protect us.
You rose like the dawn
   in answer to our prayers.
Lord, do not leave us in despair.   4

Flawless jewel of the hills, you are
  all good fortune of this village.
Whosoever kneels at your feet
  is released from the torment
  of desire, of dying.
Rest your palms like lotus petals
  upon our heads.
Lord, we surrender to you.   5

Your courage conquers misery.
Pride bows to your smile.
Accept us however you like,
  as friends or servants,
  only show us your lotus face,
  that we may kneel at your feet.   6

Your feet follow the hoofprints
  of the grazing cows.
Your feet dance upon the serpent's head.
Your feet, adored by good fortune,
  crush the sins of simple folk like us.
Step firmly upon our hearts,
  that we may be free of sorrow.   7

Your voice is tender, your words endearing.
The renounced and learned fall for you
and sacrifice. We simple milkmaids
  are fainting fools. You are our hero.
Revive us with the nectar of your song.   8

Stories of your immortal feats
   save the afflicted. Hearing these stories told
   sanctifies the sinner and sustains the saint.
Sages and poets praise you for all to hear;
   theirs is true generosity.   9

We meditate upon your glance,
   your laughter, and your stride.
Time and again, you have stolen
   away with us to touch the heart.
We would forget you, but we cannot.
Lord, show yourself.   10

When you wander off to graze the calves,
   your feet, tender as lotus petals,
   might be bruised by stones or thorns.
So, we agonize.
Lord, show yourself.   11

When you return at dusk,
   your dark curls wild,
   your face smudged with blue dust
   kicked up by the calves,
   we rejoice.
Lord, show yourself.   12

You sanctify all who surrender at your feet—
   your feet like lotus blossoms,
   your feet like jewels upon the earth.
Beloved cowherd, you are our comfort
   and our peace. Soothe
   these troubled minds.
Lord, show yourself.   13

Your lips kiss the flute and
   fill it with tremulous song.
Each note heals lust's wounds.
Let us be your flute.
End this sorrow of separation.   14

By day, you disappear into the woods.
A moment with you out of sight
   feels like eons to us.
When you return at dusk,
   curls tangled about your face,
   we drink in your gaze.
Then, how cruel seems
   the blinking of our eyes.   15

We left husbands and sons. Yes, we
   renounced our families for the music
   of your flute, but now you've abandoned
   us—for what? Lord, show yourself.   16

We long to linger alone with you.
Our hearts rise at the thought
   of your laughter, of your sidelong glance.
We would lay our heads upon your chest.
We have lost our minds to you.
Lord, show yourself.   17

A glimpse of you relieves
   the longings of all who dwell
   in this village—cowherds, swans,
   monkeys, peacocks, calves,
   and maidens, alike.
A glimpse of you blesses
   this entire creation.
Without you, we are heartsick.
Give us the antidote.
Lord, show yourself.   18

Now, your tender feet may be bruised
  by stone and thorn.
We would hold them gently
  and rest them upon our hearts.
Lord, we live only for you.   19

—*Srimad Bhagavatam* X.31

॥श्री मधुराष्टकम्॥

अधरं मधुरं वदनं मधुरम्
नयनं मधुरं हसितं मधुरम् ।
हृदयं मधुरं गमनं मधुरम्
मधुराधिपतेरखिलं मधुरम् ॥ १ ॥

वचनं मधुरं चरितं मधुरम्
वसनं मधुरं वलितं मधुरम् ।
चलितं मधुरं भ्रमितं मधुरम्
मधुराधिपतेरखिलं मधुरम् ॥ २ ॥

वेणुर्मधुरो रेणुर्मधुरः
पाणिर्मधुरः पादौ मधुरौ ।
नृत्यं मधुरं सख्यं मधुरम्
मधुराधिपतेरखिलं मधुरम् ॥ ३ ॥

गीतं मधुरं पीतं मधुरम्
भुक्तं मधुरं सुप्तं मधुरम् ।
रूपं मधुरं तिलकं मधुरम्
मधुराधिपतेरखिलं मधुरम् ॥ ४ ॥

करणं मधुरं तरणं मधुरम्
हरणं मधुरं रमणं मधुरम् ।
वमितं मधुरं शमितं मधुरम्
मधुराधिपतेरखिलं मधुरम् ॥५॥

गुंजा मधुरा माला मधुरा
यमुना मधुरा वीचिर्मधुरा ।
सलिलं मधुरं कमलं मधुरम्
मधुराधिपतेरखिलं मधुरम् ॥६॥

गोपी मधुरा लीला मधुरा
युक्तं मधुरं मुक्तं मधुरम् ।
इष्टं मधुरं शिष्टं मधुरम्
मधुराधिपतेरखिलं मधुरम् ॥७॥

गोपा मधुरा गावो मधुरा
यष्टिर्मधुरा सृष्टिर्मधुरा ।
दलितं मधुरं फलितं मधुरम्
मधुराधिपतेरखिलं मधुरम् ॥८॥

SRI MADHURASTAKAM

Sweet is his pout, sweet is his face,
  sweet are his eyes, sweet is his laugh,
  sweet is his heart, sweet is his stroll—
All is sweet about the Lord who is sweet.   1

Sweet is his word, sweet is his deed,
  sweet is his cloth, sweet is his stance,
  sweet is his wandering, sweet is his loss—
All is sweet about the Lord who is sweet.   2

Sweet is his flute, sweet is his dust,
  sweet is his touch, sweet are his feet,
  sweet is his dance, sweet is his bond—
All is sweet about the Lord who is sweet.   3

Sweet is his song, sweet is his drink,
  sweet is his food, sweet is his sleep,
  sweet is his form, sweet is his mark—
All is sweet about the Lord who is sweet.   4

Sweet is his teasing, sweet is his triumph,
  sweet is his stealing, sweet is his dallying,
  sweet is his refusal, sweet is his promise—
All is sweet about the Lord who is sweet.   5

Sweet are his berries, sweet are his flowers,
  sweet is his Yamuna, sweet are his ripples,
  sweet is his splashing, sweet is his lotus—
All is sweet about the Lord who is sweet.   6

Sweet are his milkmaids, sweet is his frolic,
  sweet is his union, sweet is his freedom,
  sweet is his glance, sweet is his courting—
All is sweet about the Lord who is sweet.   7

Sweet are his cowherds, sweet are his cows,
  sweet is his goad, sweet is his grace,
  sweet is his ripening, sweet is his bliss—
All is sweet about the Lord who is sweet.   8

—Sri Vallabhacarya

॥ श्री हनुमान चालीसा ॥

दोहा

श्री गुरु चरन सरोज रज
निज मनु मुकुरु सुधारि ।
बरन-उँ रघुबर बिमल जसु
जो दायकु फल चारि ॥

बुद्धि हीन तनु जानिके
सुमिरौं पवन कुमार ।
बल बुद्धि विद्या देहु मोहिं
हरहु कलेस बिकार ॥

चौप-ई

जय हनुमान ज्ञान गुन सागर ।
जय कपीस तिहुँ लोक उजागर ॥
रामदूत अतुलित बल धामा ।
अञ्जनि पुत्र पवनसुत नामा ॥ १-२ ॥

महाबीर बिक्रम बजरङ्गी ।
कुमति निवार सुमति के सङ्गी ॥
कञ्चन बरन बिराज सुबेस ।
कानन कुंडल कुञ्चित केसा ॥३-४॥

हाथ बज्र और ध्वजा बिराजै ।
कँधे मूँज जने-उ साजै ॥
शङ्कर सुवन केसरी नन्दन ।
तेज प्रताप महा जग बन्दन ॥५-६॥

विद्यावान गुणी अति चातुर ।
राम काज करिबे को आतुर ॥
प्रभु चरित्र सुनिबे को रसिया ।
राम लखन सीता मन बसिया ॥७-८॥

सूक्ष्म रुप धरि सियहिं दिखावा ।
बिकट रुप धरि लङ्क जरावा ॥
भीम रुप धरि असुर सँहारे ।
रामचन्द्र के काज सँवारे ॥९-१०॥

लाय सञ्जीवन लखन जियाये ।

श्री रघुबीर हरषि उर लाये ॥

रघुपति कीन्ही बहुत बरा-ई ।

तुम मम प्रिय भरतहि सम भा-ई ॥११-१२॥

सहस बदन तुम्हरो जस गावै ।

अस कहि श्रीपति कण्ठ लगावै ॥

सनकादिक ब्रह्मादि मुनीसा ।

नारद शारद सहित अहिसा ॥१३-१४॥

यम कुबेर दिगपाल जहाँ ते ।

कबि कोबिद कहि सके कहां ते ॥

तुम उपकार सुग्रीवहिं कीन्हा ।

राम मिलाय राजपद दीन्हा ॥१५-१६॥

तुम्हरो मन्त्र विभीषण माना ।

लङ्केश्वर भये सब जग जाना ॥

युग सहस्र योजन पर भानू ।

लील्यो ताहि मधुर फल जानू ॥१७-१८॥

प्रभु मुद्रिका मेलि मुख माहीं ।

जलधि लाँघि गये अचरज नाहीं ॥

दुर्गम काज जगत के जेते ।

सुगम अनुग्रह तुम्हरे तेते ॥१९-२०॥

राम दुआरे तुम रखवारे ।

होत न आज्ञा बिनु पैसारे ॥

सब सुख लहै तुम्हारी सरना ।

तुम रक्षक काहू को डरना ॥२१-२२॥

आपन तेज सम्हारो आपै ।

तीनों लोक हाँक ते काँपै ॥

भूत पिसाच निकट नहीं आवै ।

महाबीर जब नाम सुनावै ॥२३-२४॥

नासै रोग हरे सब पीरा ।

जपत निरन्तर हनुमत बीरा ॥

सङ्कट तें हनुमान छुड़ावै ।

मन क्रम बचन ध्यान जो लावै ॥२५-२६॥

सब पर राम तपस्वी राजा ।

तिन के काज सकल तुम साजा ॥

और मनोरथ जो को-ई लावै ।

सो-ई अमित जीवन फल पावै ॥२७-२८॥

चारों जुग परताप तुम्हारा ।

है परसिद्ध जगत उजियारा ॥

साधु सन्त के तुम रखवारे ।

असुर निकन्दन राम दुलारे ॥२९-३०॥

अष्ट सिद्धि नौ निधि के दाता ।

अस बर दीन जानकी माता ॥

राम रसायन तुम्हरे पासा ।

सद रहो रघुपति के दासा ॥३१-३२॥

तुम्हरे भजन राम को पावै ।

जनम जनम के दुख बिसरावै ॥

अन्त काल रघुबर पुर जा-ई ।

जहाँ जन्म हरि भक्त कहा-ई ॥३३-३४॥

और देवता चित्त न धर-ई ।
हनुमत से-इ सर्व सुख कर-ई ॥
सङ्कट कटै मिटै सब पीरा ।
जो सुमिरै हनुमत बल बीरा ॥ ३५-३६ ॥

जय जय जय हनुमान गोसा-ईं ।
कृपा करहु गुरुदेव की ना-ईं ॥
जो सत बार पाठ कर को-ई ।
छूटहि बंदि महा सुख हो-ई ॥ ३७-३८ ॥

जो यह पढ़ै हनुमान चालीसा ।
होय सिद्धि साखि गौरीसा ॥
तुलसिदास सदा हरि चेरा ।
कीजै नाथ हृदय महँ डेरा ॥ ३९-४० ॥

दोहा

पवनतनय सङ्कट हरन ।
मङ्गल मूरति रुप ॥
राम लखन सीता सहित ।
हृदय बसहु सुर भूप ॥

HANUMAN CHALISA

I take refuge in the dust of the guru's holy feet
  to polish the mirror of the heart.
So, I prepare to sing the glories
  of the father of the Raghu dynasty.
Devotion bestows all that is good in life:
  virtue, prosperity, joy, and freedom.

I am not learned,
  but I supplicate the great Hanuman
  to bless me in these efforts.
Son of the wind,
  flood me with courage, intelligence,
  and your eternal grace,
  that I may praise you with all my heart.
I offer to you my sorrows and failings.

Hail to the feet of Sita's Lord Ram.

Victory to you, Hanuman, ocean of light.
Victory to you, monkey king
  who is adored throughout time and space,
  mind and dream, and that which can never
  be known.
Carrying Lord Ram's message,
  you are the hero of all time.
None can match your power, son of Anjani,
  you who are said to be the wind's child.   1-2

Hanuman, you are bold and fearless
  like a sudden bolt of lightning.
Your light liberates the mind.
You are a faithful companion,
  the most desirable company.   3

Strong, you are adorned with splendid silks,
  bright earrings, and long, curly locks;
  you glow, golden with the light of compassion. 4

You wield mace and flag,
  and wear a simple sacred thread
  across your shoulders.
Son of Sankara and Kesari,
  you are the boon bestowed by Lord Siva.   5-6

You are the wellspring
  of wisdom, wit, and virtue,
  humbly devoted to Lord Ram.   7

Drinking in stories
  of your beloved Lord
  like nectar,
  you live forever
  in the hearts of Sri Ram,
  his brother Laksman,
  and his wife, Mother Sita.   8

In tiny form, you humbled yourself
   before Queen Sita;
   yet to the demon leader,
   you appeared with great force
   and burnt his city Lanka to the ground.   9

In wrathful form, you slew
   the army of fiends, as heartfelt service
   to the Lord of righteousness.   10

You procured the elixir of life,
   sacred mountain herb,
   to revive Laksman.
   So, Lord Ram embraced you
   and said, "You are like a brother
   to me, my very kin.
   Forever, may thousands
   praise your name."   11-12

Of the countless saints and sages,
   gods, scholars, and poets,
   none can relate your true limitless glory.
Not Sanaka, Brahma, Narada, Sarada,
   or even Lord Vishnu's serpent throne.   13-14

Still, they praise you—
   the Lords of death and wealth.
The wind, she sings your name
   from all directions.   15

Sugriva, leader of the monkey tribe,
   followed you to the feet of Lord Ram
   who then named him king.   16

Vibhisana, brother of the demon king,
   revered your word,
   and so ruled over Lanka.   17

You sprang up a thousand miles
   into the sky and swallowed the sun
   like a sweet golden fruit.
You carried Lord Ram's ring in your mouth
   and leapt easily across the ocean.
Nothing is impossible
   with your ever-flowing grace.   18-20

You are the keeper of Lord Ram's door.
None may enter without your grace.   21

You are the refuge of all blessings.
Those who love you know no fear.
Only you radiate such glory.
The universe trembles
   at the sound of your voice.   22

Ghosts, demons, and troublesome spirits
   shudder and disband
   when your name is called.   23-24

Nor can pain or illness
   withstand the sound.   25

One who thinks only of you,
   whose every breath and deed
   is offered in your name
   will be liberated, forever.   26

Lord Ram embodies righteousness.
You bring his word to life.
Whosoever bows down before you,
   seeking with a sincere heart,
   is blessed with utter and eternal
   fulfillment.   27-28

Your glory lights the ages of
   gold, silver, bronze, and iron.
The breath of the universe
   is the sound of your name.   29

You protect tradition,
   as guardian of *sadhus*,
   destroyer of demons,
   most tender devotee of Lord Ram.   30

The eight *siddhis* and nine *nidhis*,
   all power and treasure,
   are yours to grant,
   by the blessed boon of Mother Sita.   31

You heal with the elixir
   of Lord Ram's name.
Forever will you remain devoted,
   lifting the burdens
   of true and helpless seekers,
   lifetime after lifetime.   32

In singing your praises,
   one is reunited with Lord Ram,
   relieved of countless sufferings
   and of future rebirth.
Such a one, at death, will either
   go to the glorious city of Lord Ram,
   or be reborn in this world
   as his most humble servant.   33-34

One need think of nothing else,
   for dearest Hanuman,
   you bestow all delight.   35

Pain and suffering vanish
   when your strength and glory
   are remembered.   36

Yes! Yes! Yes! Lord Hanuman is victorious.
Let your grace flood through me,
   beloved *guru*.   37

One who sings these verses
   from memory
   one hundred times
   is freed from meaningless desires
   and discovers within the greatest joy.   38

One who recites these verses daily
   will be blessed with perfection,
   as Lord Siva is witness.   39

Tulsidas, eternal servant of beloved Hari, says,
   "Lord, make your home in my heart, forever."   40

Son of the wind,
  destroyer of sorrows,
  embodiment of all blessings,
  with Lord Ram, Laksman, and Mother Sita,
  live ever enshrined in my heart.

—Sri Tulsidas

NOTES
This translation was written on Hanuman Jayanti, 2009. It has
been reprinted with permission from literary journal *Lalitamba*
(Issue 4; Chintamani Books, 2011).

॥ लिङ्गाष्टकम् ॥

ब्रह्म मुरारि सुरार्चित लिङ्गं
निर्मल भासित शोभित लिङ्गम् ।
जन्मज दुःख विनाशक लिङ्गम्
तत् प्रणमामि सदाशिव लिङ्गम् ॥ १ ॥

देवमुनि प्रवरार्चित लिङ्गं
कामदहन करुणाकर लिङ्गम् ।
रावण दर्प विनाशन लिङ्गं
तत् प्रणमामि सदाशिव लिङ्गम् ॥ २ ॥

सर्व सुगन्ध सुलेपित लिङ्गं
बुद्धि विवर्धन कारन लिङ्गम् ।
सिध्द सुरासुर विन्दत लिङ्गं
तत् प्रणमामि सदाशिव लिङ्गम् ॥ ३ ॥

कनक महामणि भूषित लिङ्गं
फणिपति वेष्टित शोभित लिङ्गं ।
दक्ष सुयज्ञ निनाशन लिङ्गं
तत् प्रणमामि सदाशिव लिङ्गम् ॥ ४ ॥

कुङ्कुम चन्दन लेपित लिङ्गं
पङ्कज हार सुशोभित लिङ्गम् ।
सञ्चित पाप विनाशन लिङ्गं
तत् प्रणमामि सदाशिव लिङ्गम् ॥५॥

देवगणार्चित सेवित लिङ्गं
भावैर्भक्तिभिरेव च लिङ्गम् ।
दिनकर कोटि प्रभाकर लिङ्गं
तत् प्रणमामि सदाशिव लिङ्गम् ॥६॥

अष्टदलोपरिवेष्टित लिङ्गं
सर्वसमुद्भव कारण लिङ्गम् ।
अष्टदरिद्र विनाशन लिङ्गं
तत् प्रणमामि सदाशिव लिङ्गम् ॥७॥

सुरगुरू सुरवर पूजित लिङ्गं
सुरवन पुष्प सदार्चित लिङ्गम् ।
परात्परं परमात्मक लिङ्गं
तत् प्रणमामि सदाशिव लिङ्गम् ॥८॥

लिङ्गाष्टकमिदं पुण्यं यः पठेशिव सन्निधौ ।
शिवलोकमवाप्नोति शिवेन सह मोदते ॥

LINGASTAKAM

I bow to the sacred *lingam*
  worshiped by the creator
  and the slayer of demons, alike.
Pure, praised, and resplendent,
  conquerer of bodily sorrows,
  vanquisher of suffering—
  to that sada siva lingam, I bow.   1

Adored by gods and sages,
  the *lingam* burns desire to blessed ash;
  source of mercy,
  destroyer of pride, arrogance, and conceit—
  to that sada siva lingam, I bow.   2

Honored with fragrant balms and perfumes,
  turgid wisdom,
  perfect master,
  praised even by the ignorant—
  to that sada siva lingam, I bow.   3

Decorated with golden ornaments and
  enormous, glittering jewels,
  robed in the thick coils of the serpent king,
  destroyer of pompous sacrifice—
  to that sada siva lingam, I bow.   4

Smeared with saffron and sandalwood paste,
   lotus born of mud,
   stealthy thief of sorrow,
   pure effulgence,
   the one who forgives all sin—
   to that sada siva lingam, I bow.   5

Worshipped by multitudes
   of holy and divine beings,
   mood of devotion,
   hope of the afflicted,
   most excellent radiance—
   to that sada siva lingam, I bow.   6

Tantric *cakra*,
   lotus of eight petals,
   giver of life,
   the one who uplifts the poor—
   to that sada siva lingam, I bow.   7

Benevolent parent,
   divine beloved,
   Lord
   forever worshiped with wildly
   fragrant flowers,
   immanent and transcendent presence—
   to that sada siva lingam, I bow.   8

One who reads, recites, or chants
  these eight verses in praise of Lord Siva
  and thinks always of Lord Siva,
  merges with Lord Siva and
  lives forever in delight with the Lord.

—Anonymous

NOTES
These verses are attributed by some to Sri Sankaracarya.

॥ रुद्राष्टध्यायी ॥

नमस्ते रुद्र मन्यव उतो त इषवे नमः ।
बाहुभ्यामुत ते नमः ॥ १ ॥

या ते रुद्र शिवा तनूरघोरापापकाशिनी ।
तया नस्तन्वा शंतमया गिरिशन्ताभि चाकशीहि ॥ २ ॥

यामिषुं गिरिशन्त हस्ते बिभर्ष्यस्तवे ।
शिवां गिरित्र तां कुरु मा हिँसीः पुरुषं जगत् ॥ ३ ॥

शिवेन वचसा त्वा गिरिशाच्छा वदामसि ।
यथा नः सर्वमिज्जगदयक्ष्मँ सुमना असत् ॥ ४ ॥

अध्यवोचदधिवक्ता प्रथमो दैव्यो भिषक् ।
अहीँश्च सर्वान्जम्भयन्त्सर्वाश्च यातुधान्यो धराचीः परा सुव ॥ ५ ॥

असौ यस्ताम्रो अरुण उत बभ्रुः सुमङ्गलः ।
ये चैनँ रुद्रा अभितो दिक्षु श्रिताः सहस्रशो वैषाँ हेड ईमहे ॥ ६ ॥

असौ यो वसर्पति नीलग्रीवो विलोहितः ।
उतैनं गोपा अदृश्रन्नदृश्रन्नुदहार्यः स दृष्टो मृडयाति नः ॥ ७ ॥

नमोस्तु नीलग्रीवाय सहस्राक्षाय मीढुषे ॥
अथो ये अस्य सत्वानो हं तेभ्यो करं नमः ॥८॥

प्रमुञ्च धन्वनस्त्वमुभयोराद्र्व्योर्ज्याम् ।
याश्च ते हस्त इषवः परा ता भगवो वप ॥९॥

विज्यं धनुः कपर्दिनो विशल्यो वाणवाँ उत ।
अनेशन्नस्य या इषव आभुरस्य निषङ्गधिः ॥१०॥

या ते हेतिर्मीढुष्टम हस्ते बभूव ते धनुः ।
तयास्मान्विश्वस्त्वमयक्ष्मया परि भुज ॥११॥

परि ते धन्वनो हेतिरस्मान्वृणक्तु विश्वतः ।
अथो य इषुधिस्तवारे अस्मन्नि धेहि तम् ॥१२॥

अवतत्य धनुष्ट्वँ सहस्राक्ष शतेषुधे ।
निशीर्य शल्यानां मुखा शिवो नः सुमना भव ॥१३॥

नमस्त आयुधायानाततायाधृष्णवे ।
उभाभ्यामुत ते नमो बाहुभां तव धन्वने ॥१४॥

मा नो महान्तमुत मा नो अर्भकं मा न उक्षन्तमुत मा न उक्षितम् ।
मा नो वधीः पितरं मोत मातरं मा नः प्रियास्तन्वो रुद्र रीरिषः ॥१५॥

मा नस्तोके तनये मा न आयुषि मा नो गोषु मा नो अश्वेषु रीरिषः ।

मा नो वीरान्रुद्र भामिनो वधीर्हविष्मन्तः सदमित्त्वा हवामहे ॥ १६ ॥

RUDRASTADHYAYI

I bow to you, fierce Lord Rudra.
To your arrows,
    to your shoulders and arms, I bow.   1

I bow to your sublime
benevolence,
    to you who guard us from sin
    and bless us with virtue's fruit,
    to you whose appearance dispels delusion,
    to you who rouse joy,
    to you who pervade the mountains.
Lord, shine upon us.   2

Mountain Lord, you hold
    arrows in hand. May your release
    protect mankind and creation.   3

Benevolent Lord of the mountains,
    we offer you these words of prayer.
May all of creation be free from
    illness and affliction. May we be
    of sound mind.   4

Lord, you who gave us language,
    you who revealed scripture;
    you are the primordial light
    that heals.
You crush reptilian sin and
    conquer any spirit of malevolence.   5

You are the sun—
   red in rising and setting,
   and all shades of gold.
May your blessed light arise
   in all directions,
   intimate and everywhere.
Let none be burnt by your wrath.   6

The sun in setting turns to blood, then
   gives way to your blue-throated night.
Lord, you appear to the cowherds,
   to the water-bearing maidens.
The sight of you brings ecstasy.   7

I bow to you, Lord of truth,
   light of a thousand eyes,
   you who bless us with the rains.
I bow to you and to all who adore you.   8

Lord, unstring your bow.
Cast aside the arrow that you hold.   9

Yes, Lord of matted locks,
   release your bow
   from cord and arrow.
Let the arrows be splintered,
   that your quiver rest empty.   10

Let your bow harm none
   and protect all.
Lord, bless us with the light of awakening,
   beyond illusions of birth and death.   11

Lord, let your arrows now be tossed
    aside, your quiver set down far from us.   12

With bow unstrung,
    may you of a thousand eyes
    and as many quivers
    blunt your arrow tips,
    that our minds be at ease.   13

Lord, I bow to your
    weaponry laid aside—
    the bow and arrows,
    and to your strong arms.   14

Wound not elder or youth,
    mother or infant,
    parent, beloved, or progeny.   15

Let no harm come
    to the children or grandchildren,
    to any life.
Let no harm come
    to the cows or horses,
    to the soldiers.
Lord, we cry out to you,
    ever in sacrifice.   16

—*Sukla Yajur Veda*

॥ भवान्यष्टकं ॥

न तातो न माता न बन्धुर्न दाता
न पुत्रो न पुत्री न भृत्यो न भर्ता ।
न जाया न विद्या न वृत्तिर्ममैव
गतिस्त्वं गतिस्त्वं त्वमेका भवानि ॥ १ ॥

भवाब्धावपारे महादुःखभीरु
पपात प्रकामी प्रलोभी प्रमत्तः ।
कुसंसारपाशप्रबद्धः सदाहं
गतिस्त्वं गतिस्त्वं त्वमेका भवानि ॥ २ ॥

न जानामि दानं न च ध्यानयोगं
न जानामि तन्त्रं न च स्तोत्रमन्त्रम् ।
न जानामि पूजां न च न्यासयोगं
गतिस्त्वं गतिस्त्वं त्वमेका भवानि ॥ ३ ॥

न जानामि पुण्यं न जानामि तीर्थं
न जानामि मुक्तिं लयं वा कदाचित् ।
न जानामि भक्तिं व्रतं वापि मात
गतिस्त्वं गतिस्त्वं त्वमेका भवानि ॥ ४ ॥

कुकर्मी कुसङ्गी कुबुद्धिः कुदासः
कुलाचारहीनः कदाचारलीनः ।
कुदृष्टिः कुवाक्यप्रबन्धः सदाहं
गतिस्त्वं गतिस्त्वं त्वमेका भवानि ॥५॥

प्रजेशं रमेशं महेशं सुरेशं
दिनेशं निशीथेश्वरं वा कदाचित् ।
न जानामि चान्यत् सदाहं शरण्ये
गतिस्त्वं गतिस्त्वं त्वमेका भवानि ॥ ६॥

विवादे विषादे प्रमादे प्रवासे
जले चानले पर्वते शत्रुमध्ये ।
अरण्ये शरण्ये सदा मां प्रपाहि
गतिस्त्वं गतिस्त्वं त्वमेका भवानि ॥७॥

अनाथो दरिद्रो जरारोगयुक्तो
महाक्षीणदीनः सदा जाड्यवक्रः ।
विपत्तौ प्रविष्टः प्रनष्टः सदाहं
गतिस्त्वं गतिस्त्वं त्वमेका भवानि ॥८॥

॥ इति श्रीमदादिशंकराचार्य विरचितं भवान्यष्टकं सम्पूर्णम् ॥

BHAVANYASTAKAM

No father, no mother, no brother have I.
No relation, no child, no loved one have I.
Mother, I am alone in the world.
Even this mind,
   with its victories and intellect,
   gets confused
   and cannot be counted upon.
You alone, you alone are my true refuge.   1

Mother, while seeking your truth,
   I have fallen.
Now, I am drowning
   in this ocean of sorrows.
I am afraid.
I am snared in the noose
   of lust and greed,
   caught in the wheel
   of birth and rebirth.
You alone, you alone are my true refuge.   2

Mother, I have nothing to offer.
I have not realized you in meditation.
I know no sacred rituals,
   no verses of praise,
   not even a single *mantra*.
It's true. I don't know
   how to worship you,
   and yet I need your grace.
You alone, you alone are my true refuge.   3

Mother, I don't deserve you, and
  I have no guide on this path.
I am not liberated
  or even steady in meditation.
I am not devoted to you,
   as I should be.
I don't know how to keep vows.
You alone, you alone are my true refuge.   4

Mother, I try hard, but
  I make many mistakes.
I am bereft of spiritual friends.
I am not a scholar,
  nor am I humble enough
  to serve you.
I have been accepted by no teacher.
I am confused and sorrowful.
My words may not always be pleasing.
My gaze wanders,
  for my mind is distracted.
You alone, you alone are my true refuge.   5

Mother, I know nothing
  of the shining ones.
I may not show proper respect, delight,
  awe, compassion, or even devotion.
No, I don't know much of these things.
I am just a child, your child.
You alone, you alone are my true refuge.   6

In the throes of quarrel or lust,
    when I fall reckless or leave you,
    when I am hurt,
    when there is no caring
    face to turn to,
    in the desert or wilderness—
    Mother, protect me.
Always hold me close.
You alone, you alone are my true refuge.   7

Mother, I am a beggar,
    an orphan.
I fear disease and old age.
Yes, I am afflicted with sorrow.
I feel vulnerable, and
    the world seems cold.
When I am lost,
    the only truth is you.
You alone, you alone are my true refuge.   8

—Sri Sankaracarya

॥ महिषासुर मर्दिनि स्तोत्रं ॥

अयि गिरि नंदिनि नंदित मोदिनि विश्व विनोदिनि नंदनुते
गिरि वर विंध्यशिरोधि निवासिनि विष्णुविलासिनि जिष्णुनुते ।
भगवति हे शितिकंठ कुटुंबिनि भूरिकुटुंबिनि भूरिकृते
जय जय हे महिषासुर मर्दिनि रम्यकपर्दिनि शैलसुते ॥ १ ॥

सुरवर वर्षिणि दुर्धर दर्शिनि दुर्मुख मर्शिनि हर्षरते
त्रिभुवन पोषिनि संकटरोषिनि किल्बिषमोषिणि घोषरते ।
दनुज निरोषिणि दितिसुत रोषिणि दुर्मद शोषिणि सिंधुसुते
जय जय हे महिषासुर मर्दिनि रम्यकपर्दिनि शैलसुते ॥ २ ॥

अयि जगदंब मदंब कदंब वनप्रिय वासिनि हासरते
शिखिरि शिरोमणि तुंग हिमालय शृंग निजालय मध्यगते ।
मधुमधुरे मधुकैटभगंजिनि कैटभ भंजिनि रासरते
जय जय हे महिषासुर मर्दिनि रम्यकपर्दिनि शैलसुते ॥ ३ ॥

अयि शतखंड विखंडित रुद्र वितुंडित शुंड गजाधिपते
ऋषपगजगगंड विदारणचंड पराक्रमशुंड मृगाधिपते ।
निजभुजदंड निपातित खंड विपातित मुंड भटादिपते
जय जय हे महिषासुर मर्दिनि रम्यकपर्दिनि शैलसुते ॥ ४ ॥

अयि रणदुर्मुद षट्वदोदित दुर्धर निर्जर शक्तिभृते

चतुरविकार धुरीण महाशिव दूतकृता प्रमथाधिपते ।

दुरित दुरीह दुराशय दुर्मति दानवदूत कृतांतमते

जय जय हे महिषासुर मर्दिनि रम्यकपर्दिनि शैलसुते ॥५॥

अयि शरणागत वैरि वधूवर वीर वराभयदायकृते

त्रिभुवन मस्तक शूलविरोधि शिरोधिकृतामल शूलकरे ।

दुमिदुमितामर दुंदुभिनाद महो मुखरीकृत तिगमकरे

जय जय हे महिषासुर मर्दिनि रम्यकपर्दिनि शैलसुते ॥ ६॥

अयि निजहुंकृतिमात्र निराकृत धूम्रविलोचन धुम्रशते

समरविशोशित शोणितबीज समुद्रवशोणित बीजलते ।

शिव शिव शुंभ निशुंभ महाहव तर्पित भूत पिशाचरते

जय जय हे महिषासुर मर्दिनि रम्यकपर्दिनि शैलसुते ॥७॥

धनुरनुसंग रणक्षणसंग परिस्फुरदंग नटकटके

कनक पिशंग प्रिषत्कनिसंग रसद्भट श्रृंग हतावटुके ।

कृतचतुरंग बलक्षितिरंग घटद्बहुरंग रटद्बटुके

जय जय हे महिषासुर मर्दिनि रम्यकपर्दिनि शैलसुते ॥८॥

जय जय जप्यजये जय शब्दपरस्तुति तत्पर विश्वनुते

झण झण झिंझिमि झिंकृतनूपुर सिंजितमोहित भूतपते ।

नटितनटार्ध नटीनटनायक नटीतनाठ्य सुगानरते

जय जय हे महिषासुर मर्दिनि रम्यकपर्दिनि शैलसुते ॥९॥

अयि सुमनः सुमनः सुमनः सुमनः सुमनोहर कांतियुते
श्रितरजनी रजनी रजनी रजनी रजनीकर वक्त्रवृते ।
सुनयन विभ्रमर भ्रमर भ्रमर भ्रमर भ्रमराधिपते
जय जय हे महिषासुर मर्दिनि रम्यकपर्दिनि शैलसुते ॥ १० ॥

सहित महाहव मल्लम तल्लिक मल्लित रल्लक मल्लरते
विरचित वल्लित पल्लिक मल्लिक झिल्लिक भिल्लिक वर्गवृते ।
सितकृतफुल्लि समुल्ल सितारुण तल्लज पल्लव सल्ललिते
जय जय हे महिषासुर मर्दिनि रम्यकपर्दिनि शैलसुते ॥ ११ ॥

अविरल गंड गलन्मद मेदुर मत्तमतंगज राजपते
त्रिभुवन भूषण भूतकलानिधि रुप पयोनिधि राजसुते ।
अयि उदतीजन लालसमानस मोहन मन्मथ राजसुते
जय जय हे महिषासुर मर्दिनि रम्यकपर्दिनि शैलसुते ॥ १२ ॥

कमलदलामल कोमलकांति कलाकलितामल भाललते
सकलविलास कलानिलयक्रम केलिचटालक हंसकुले ।
अलिकुलसंकल कुवलयमंडल मौलिमिलाद्धकुलालिकुले
जय जय हे महिषासुर मर्दिनि रम्यकपर्दिनि शैलसुते ॥ १३ ॥

करमुरलीरव वीजित कूजित लज्जित कोकिल मंजुमते
मिलितपुलिंद मनोहरगुंजित रंजितशैल निकुंजगते ।
निजगुणभूत महाशबरीगण सद्गुण संभृत केलिलते
जय जय हे महिषासुर मर्दिनि रम्यकपर्दिनि शैलसुते ॥ १४ ॥

कटितटपीत दुकूलविचित्र मयूख तिरस्कृत चंद्ररुचे
प्रणतसुरासुर मौलिमणस्फुर दंशुल सनख चंद्ररुचे ।
जितकनकाचल मौलिपदोर्चित निर्भरकुंजर कुंभकुचे
जय जय हे महिषासुर मर्दिनि रम्यकपर्दिनि शैलसुते ॥१५॥

विजतसहस्र करैक सहस्र करैक सहस्र करैकनुते
कृतसुरतारक संगरतारक संगरतारक सूनसुते ।
सुरथसमाधि समानसमाधि समाधि समाधि सुजातरते
जय जय हे महिषासुर मर्दिनि रम्यकपर्दिनि शैलसुते ॥१६॥

पदकमलाम करुणानिलये वरि वस्यति योऽनुदिनम स शिवे
अयि कमले कमलानिलये कमलानिलयः स कथं ने भवेत् ।
तव पदमेव परम पदमेव नुशीलतये मम किम न शिवे
जय जय हे महिषासुर मर्दिनि रम्यकपर्दिनि शैलसुते ॥१७॥

कनकलसत्कल सिंधु जलैरनुसिंचिनुते गुणरंगभुवम
भजति स किम् न शचिकुचकुंभ तटीपरिरंभ सुखानुभवम ।
तव चरणं शरणं करवाणी नतामरवाणी निवासी शिवम्
जय जय हे महिषासुर मर्दिनि रम्यकपर्दिनि शैलसुते ॥१८॥

तव विमलेंदुकुलं वदनेंदुमलं सकलं ननु कूलयते
किमु पुरूहूत पुरींदुमुखि सुमुखीभिरसौ विमुखीक्रियते ।
ममतु मतं शिवनामधने भवति कृपया किमुत क्रियते
जय जय हे महिषासुर मर्दिनि रम्यकपर्दिनि शैलसुते ॥१९॥

अयि मयि दीनदयालुतया कृपवैव तया भवितव्यमुमे
अयि जगतो जननि कृपयासि यतासि तथाऽनुमितासिरते ।
यदुचितमत्र भवत्युररी कुरुतदुरुत पमपाकुरुते
जय जय हे महिषासुर मर्दिनि रम्यकपर्दिनि शैलसुते ॥ २० ॥

MAHISASURA MARDINI STOTRAM

Dear daughter of the mountain
  who makes the earth fertile
  and delights the universe,
  you who roam low hills
  even as you dwell on the peak,
  playmate of Visnu,
  victorious goddess,
  wife of the blue-throated Lord,
  mother to all—
Victory to you!
You conquer the buffalo demon with ease,
  wearing your hair in a pleasing braid,
  dear daughter of the mountain.   1

Dear daughter of the mountain
  who rains blessings on the gods,
  tames the unruly, and is
  patient with the foul-mouthed,
  you bring all joys.
Daughter of abundance,
  you are Lord Siva's contentment.
You plunder faults,
  even as you respond to cries of distress.
Courageous girl
  who defeats anger and arrogance,
  you worship like a flooding river—
Victory to you!
You conquer the buffalo demon with ease,
  wearing your hair in a pleasing braid,
  dear daughter of the mountain.   2

Universal and rapturous mother,
  fragrant orange blossom,
  beloved who laughs aloud
  in the thick of the forest,
  crest jewel,
  Himalayan peak,
  taste of honey,
  lovely one who defeats demons,
  you worship and rejoice—
Victory to you!
You conquer the buffalo demon with ease,
  wearing your hair in a pleasing braid,
  dear daughter of the mountain.   3

Dear daughter who cracks
  the skulls of the ignorant,
  you behead those swollen with pride.
You are brave, riding the noble lion
  that crouches and springs.
You push through elephant
  cheeks and trunks.
  Immersed in battle,
  you are alluring.
You leave ascetics of
  shaven head and staff
  in the dust.
Lord, warrior, and slave
  are alike to you,
  for you fracture class structure—
Victory to you!
You conquer the buffalo demon with ease,
  wearing your hair in a pleasing braid,
  dear daughter of the mountain.   4

PETALS AT YOUR FEET

Dear daughter of endless strength,
   you delight in defeating foes—
   drunken infatuation,
   foolish pride,
   bloated arrogance.
Young girl so charming,
   you elicit support
   from your Lord's attendant,
   he who is skilled and clever in battle.
He cuts through
   the dangers of the field,
   the weakness of an ignorant mind—
Victory to you!
You conquer the buffalo demon with ease,
   wearing your hair in a pleasing braid,
   dear daughter of the mountain.   5

Dear daughter,
   you give refuge to the enemy,
   the hero, and the innocent, alike.
Your compassion relieves the three worlds
   of fear, even as you stand ready
   to spear with your glance
   those embroiled in strife,
   those whose ignorance brings pain.
Fiery one, passionate girl,
   your Lord's drumbeat rouses you.
You are like a thunderbolt—
Victory to you!
You conquer the buffalo demon with ease,
   wearing your hair in a pleasing braid,
   dear daughter of the mountain.   6

Dear daughter, your breath is primordial sound,
  elemental *mantra*.
Girl of smoky eyes,
  you eradicate sin with a sidelong glance.
You are a blood-red jewel.
You are the flowering
  vine that revives your Lord.
He is satisfied by such great acts
  as your slaying the demons of duality—
Victory to you!
You conquer the buffalo demon with ease,
  wearing your hair in a pleasing braid,
  dear daughter of the mountain.   7

Dearest girl, before battle begins
  you dance and shiver,
  your limbs adorned
  with all manner of ornament.
Holding bow in hand,
  you pull arrows
  from a quiver of burnished gold
  to fell fearsome mountain warriors.
Battle is no more
  than a colorful play to you,
  such joyous drama—
Victory to you!
You conquer the buffalo demon with ease,
  wearing your hair in a pleasing braid,
  dear daughter of the mountain.   8

Victory to soft prayers of surrender.
Victory. Victory to exuberant cries
   that ring with your highest praise.
The universe is utterly devoted to you,
   you whose tinkling anklets infatuate the Lord;
   you dance with him until the world
   disappears,
   reappears,
   disappears.
You delight all with playful song and dance—
Victory to you!
You conquer the buffalo demon with ease,
   wearing your hair in a pleasing braid,
   dear daughter of the mountain.   9

Darling blossom, sweet flower,
   your petals enchant the mind.
Your loveliness shines in the darkness,
   like the full moon illuminating the night.
You are resplendent.
Your gentle glance attracts
   devotees and the Lord, alike,
   as if they were black bees,
   buzzing bees,
   bees seeking nectar.
Sweet flower—
Victory to you!
You conquer the buffalo demon with ease,
   wearing your hair in a pleasing braid,
   dear daughter of the mountain.   10

In the company of strong men,
   you wage war,
   you, vulnerable like a deer.
You are the delight of heroes.
You live amid jasmine blossoms
   and dance to the cricket's song.
You shine in the dark of night,
   like the moon of spring tides,
   coquettish,
   with face half-veiled.
At dawn, you bloom.
Tender virgin,
   beautiful goddess Lalita—
Victory to you!
You conquer the buffalo demon with ease,
   wearing your hair in a pleasing braid,
   dear daughter of the mountain.   11

Your cries are rapturous music,
   your thighs like elephant cheeks;
   you are a leader of elephant herds,
Lustrous ornament of the three worlds,
   most precious jewel of the Lord,
   you are the fullness of the moon.
Affectionate girl,
   you give bountifully, yet you excite longing.
You are more bewildering
   than the scent of jasmine.
You agitate the mind—
Victory to you!
You conquer the buffalo demon with ease,
   wearing your hair in a pleasing braid,
   dear daughter of the mountain.   12

Dear daughter,
   you are pure like the lotus petal.
You of melodious murmur and gentle brow,
   you who sport and play with swans,
   you are graceful. Like the waterlily,
   you reveal your delicate splendor
   in the moonlight.
Devotees throng to you,
   as bees swarm to the flowering tree.
Blossom of intoxicating breath—
Victory to you!
You conquer the buffalo demon with ease,
   wearing your hair in a pleasing braid,
   dear daughter of the mountain.   13

Dear daughter,
   the call of your flute
   shames the nightingale's song.
You are to be found in the mountains,
   among those whose cry is primitive.
You are captivating,
   cavorting with the wildest women,
   who soon reflect your elegance—
Victory to you!
You conquer the buffalo demon with ease,
   wearing your hair in a pleasing braid,
   dear daughter of the mountain.   14

Dear daughter,
   with hips wrapped in yellow silk,
   your curves are shimmering hillocks.
Such radiance brings the moon to shine.
Simple girl,
   your toenails are like the moon,
   reflecting the diadem light of kings and gods
   who bow down and take refuge in you.
All find strength at your tender feet—
Victory to you!
You conquer the buffalo demon with ease,
   wearing your hair in a pleasing braid,
   dear daughter of the mountain.   15

You outshine the sun of a thousand rays.
You are more brilliant than a thousand suns
   and praised by the rays of a thousand suns.
You liberate the gods.
Luminous savior,
   shining protector,
   splendid charioteer,
   you turn all toward *samadhi.*
You are *samadhi.*
You proclaim all that is beautiful.
Samadhi! Samadhi! Samadhi!—
Victory to you!
You conquer the buffalo demon with ease,
   wearing your hair in a pleasing braid,
   dear daughter of the mountain.   16

All compassion resides at your lotus feet.
You are the source of bliss and all that is blessed.
You in whom the lotus dwells,
 you who sit upon the full-blown lotus,
 if I were to surrender completely
 at your feet,
 at your holy feet,
 would there be anything left to realize?—
Victory to you!
You conquer the buffalo demon with ease,
 wearing your hair in a pleasing braid,
 dear daughter of the mountain.   17

Dear daughter,
 your form is worshiped with light,
 sandalwood, song, and water,
 yet you are the spacious sky.
Whoever is intimate with your breasts,
 full like pitchers,
 experiences sweet bliss.
One who bows down
 to take refuge at your feet
 finds eternal life.
Your feet are the abode of the Lord—
Victory to you!
You conquer the buffalo demon with ease,
 wearing your hair in a pleasing braid,
 dear daughter of the mountain.   18

Dear one of radiant face,
  you are praised by all.
I yearn to be yours.
You of face like the stainless moon,
  you of sweet countenance,
  would you turn away from my plea?
You are indeed my mother.
The Lord calls out your name.
Shed your grace upon me, too—
Victory to you!
You conquer the buffalo demon with ease,
  wearing your hair in a pleasing braid,
  dear daughter of the mountain.   19

Sweet child, you overflow
  with compassion for the sorrowful;
  flood me with your grace.
Dear mother of all being,
  in your mercy,
  let me call you my mother.
Please smile upon this seeker,
  though I am not selfless enough
  to love you as I should,
  for only you can remove such affliction—
Victory to you!
You conquer the buffalo demon with ease,
  wearing your hair in a pleasing braid,
  dear daughter of the mountain.   20

—Sri Sankaracarya

॥ श्री ललिता सहस्रनाम ध्यानम् ॥

सिन्दूरारुणविग्रहां त्रिनयनां माणिक्यमौलिस्फुरत्

तारानायकशेखरां स्मितमुखीमापीनवक्षोरुहाम् ।

पाणिभामलिपूर्णरत्नचषकं रक्तोत्पलं बिभ्रतीं

सौम्यां रत्नघटस्थरक्तचरणां ध्यायेत्परामम्बिकाम् ॥

ध्यायेत् पद्मासनस्थां विकसितवदनां पद्मपत्रायताक्षीं

हेमाभां पीतवस्त्रां करकलितलसद् हेमपद्मां वराङ्गीम् ।

सर्वालङ्कारयुक्तां सततमभयदां भक्तनम्रां भवानीं

श्रीविद्यां शान्तमूर्तिं सकलसुररनुतां सर्वसम्पत्प्रदात्रीम् ॥

सकुङ्कुमविलेपनामलिकचुम्बिकस्तूरिकां

समन्दहसितेक्षणां सशरचापपाशाङ्कुशाम् ।

अशेषजनमोहिनीमरुणमाल्यभूषाम्बरां

जपाकुसुमभासुरां जपविधौ स्मरेदम्बिकाम् ॥

अरुणां करुणातरङ्गिताक्षीं

धृतपशाङ्कुशपुष्पबाणचापाम् ।

अणिमादिभिरावृतां मयूखैः

अहमित्येव विभावये भवानीम् ॥

SRI LALITA SAHASRANAMA DHYANAM

I meditate upon the divine mother
   who glows with the red light of dawn.
She oversees all, wearing the crescent
   moon in her crown of infinite rubies.
Her smile is ever more enticing than
   her full breasts, though both nourish the world.
She sips from a jeweled cup of nectar.
She glances fondly at the red lotus of long stem
   that blooms in the warmth of her hand.
In a pot at her feet shines all wealth,
   for those whose love is true.

Let the mind rest in the lap of the fair one,
   seated upon the great lotus of silence.
Her face is radiant with bliss,
   her glance, gentle and sidelong.
She wears golden silk
   and glows with golden light.
In her hand, she holds the golden lotus.
She is the compassionate protectress,
   beautiful to gaze upon and ever to be adored.
One is at peace in her presence.

This goddess is like a gorgeous flower:
As bees seek nectar, so devotees swarm to her.
Her fragrance soothes the mind.
She who holds noose and goad,
   bow and arrows—
   none can resist her charm.

She is adorned with offerings
  of garland and gemstone,
  with saffron powder of deepest red;
  yet she outshines all ornament.
She is a rose in full bloom.

She is the great empress, the first rising light.
Her eyes flood the world with compassion.
Her love is captivating,
  even as she urges the seeker
  to turn within.
She knows all beings as the one.

—Sri Lalita Sahasranama

॥ ॐ जय जगदीश हरे ॥

ॐ जय जगदीश हरे
स्वामी जय जगदीश हरे ।
भक्त जनों के संकट
दास जनों के संकट ।
क्षण में दूर करे ॥
ॐ जय जगदीश हरे ॥

जो ध्यावे फल पावे
दुख बिनसे मन का
स्वामी दुख बिनसे मन का ।
सुख सम्पति घर आवे
सुख सम्पति घर आवे
कष्ट मिटे तन का ।
ॐ जय जगदीश हरे ॥

ॐ जय जगदीश हरे
स्वामी जय जगदीश हरे ।
भक्त जनों के संकट
दास जनों के संकट ।
क्षण में दूर करे ॥
ॐ जय जगदीश हरे ॥

मात पिता तुम मेरे

शरण गहूं मैं किसकी

स्वामी शरण गहूं मैं किसकी

तुम बिन और न दूजा

तुम बिन और न दूजा

आस करूं मैं जिसकी ।

ॐ जय जगदीश हरे ॥

ॐ जय जगदीश हरे

स्वामी जय जगदीश हरे ।

भक्त जनों के संकट

दास जनों के संकट ।

क्षण में दूर करे ॥

ॐ जय जगदीश हरे ॥

तुम पूरण परमात्मा

तुम अंतरयामी

स्वामी तुम अंतरयामी ।

पारब्रह्म परमेश्वर

पारब्रह्म परमेश्वर

तुम सब के स्वामी ।

ॐ जय जगदीश हरे ॥

ॐ जय जगदीश हरे
स्वामी जय जगदीश हरे ।
भक्त जनों के संकट
दास जनों के संकट ।
क्षण में दूर करे ॥
ॐ जय जगदीश हरे ॥

तुम करुणा के सागर
तुम पालनकर्ता
स्वामी तुम पालनकर्ता ।
मैं मूरख खल कामी
मैं सेवक तुम स्वामी
कृपा करो भर्ता ।
ॐ जय जगदीश हरे ॥

ॐ जय जगदीश हरे
स्वामी जय जगदीश हरे ।
भक्त जनों के संकट
दास जनों के संकट ।
क्षण में दूर करे ॥
ॐ जय जगदीश हरे ॥

तुम हो एक अगोचर

सबके प्राणपति

स्वामी सबके प्राणपति ।

किस विधि मिलूं दयामय

किस विधि मिलूं कृपामय

तुमको मैं कुमति ।

ॐ जय जगदीश हरे ॥

ॐ जय जगदीश हरे

स्वामी जय जगदीश हरे ।

भक्त जनों के संकट

दास जनों के संकट ।

क्षण में दूर करे ॥

ॐ जय जगदीश हरे ॥

दीनबंधु दुखहर्ता

ठाकुर तुम मेरे

स्वामी ठाकुर तुम मेरे ।

अपने हाथ उठा-ओ

अपने शरण लगा-ओ

द्वर पड़ा तेरे ॥

ॐ जय जगदीश हरे ॥

ॐ जय जगदीश हरे

स्वामी जय जगदीश हरे ।

भक्त जनों के संकट

दास जनों के संकट ।

क्षण में दूर करे ॥

ॐ जय जगदीश हरे ॥

विषय विकार मिटा-ओ

पाप हरो देवा

स्वामी पाप हरो देवा ।

श्रद्धा भक्ति बढ़ा-ओ

श्रद्धा भक्ति बढ़ा-ओ

संतन की सेवा ।

ॐ जय जगदीश हरे ॥

ॐ जय जगदीश हरे

स्वामी जय जगदीश हरे ।

भक्त जनों के संकट

दास जनों के संकट ।

क्षण में दूर करे ॥

ॐ जय जगदीश हरे ॥

JAYA JAGADISA HARE

Victory to you, O Lord of creation.
Master to all, victory to you.
You are the mighty Lord of creation.
The perils of the faithful
   and the trials of your servants,
   you dispel in an instant.
O, hail to you, Lord of creation.   1

One who meditates upon you
   receives the fruit—
   a mind free of sorrow.
Yes, a mind free of sorrow.
Joy and abundance fill the home.
Even the body thrives, healthy.
O, hail to you, Lord of creation.   2

You are father and mother to me.
You are my true refuge.
My true refuge, you are.
Without you, there is nothing else.
Lord, you are everything to me—
I long for nothing but you.
O, hail to you, Lord of creation.   3

You are the soul of my soul.
Yes, you know my heart well.
Master, how you know all hearts.
Beyond the great beyond,
   you are the absolute Lord.
Yes, beyond, beyond, beyond,
   you are the ultimate truth.
You are the Master of all being.
O, hail to you, Lord of creation.   4

You are the sea of mercy.
You are the doer of deeds.
Master, not I but you do all.
Still, I am confused by desire.
Let me be a servant,
   that you may master the mind.
Bless me with your grace, Lord.
O, hail to you, Lord of creation.   5

You cannot be seen in this world,
   yet you protect the life of creation.
Master, you protect the life force in all.
How can I realize you?
How can I, merciful Lord?
I am lost in confusion.
O, hail to you, Lord of creation.   6

You are brother to the sorrowful,
   relieving worldly misery.
Master, you are my savior.
You are my teacher.
Raise your hand in blessing.
I pray, give me solace.
I surrender at your doorstep,
   at your feet.
O, hail to you, Lord of creation.   8

Relieve me of my faults.
Take my sins, you who shine.
Master, take my sins, for you shine.
Bless me with faith and devotion.
Yes, bless me with faith and devotion.
Forever, may I serve you.
O, hail to you, Lord of creation.   9

Victory to you, O Lord of creation.
Master to all, victory to you.
You are the almighty ruler of this world.
The perils of the faithful
   and the trials of your servants,
     you dispel in an instant.
O, hail to you, Lord of creation.   10

—Pandit Shardha Ram Phillauri

ATMA BODHA

॥आत्म बोध॥

तपोभिः क्षीणपापानां शान्तानां वीतरागिणाम् ।
मुमुक्षूणामपेक्ष्योऽयम् आत्मबोधो विधीयते ॥ १ ॥

बोधोऽन्यसाधनेभ्यो हि साक्षान्मोक्षैकसाधनम् ।
पाकस्य वह्निवज्ज्ञानं विना मोक्षो न सिध्यति ॥ २ ॥

अविरोधितया कर्म नाविद्यां विनिवर्तयेत् ।
विद्याविद्यां निहन्त्येव तेजस्तिमिरसङ्घवत् ॥ ३ ॥

परिच्छिन्न इवाज्ञानात् तन्नाशे सति केवलः ।
स्वयं प्रकाशते ह्यात्मा मेघापायेंऽशुमानिव ॥ ४ ॥

अज्ञानकलुषं जीवं ज्ञानाभ्यासाद्विनिर्मलम् ।
कृत्वा ज्ञानं स्वयं नश्येज्जलं कतकरेणुवत् ॥ ५ ॥

संसारः स्वप्नतुल्यो हि रागद्वेषादिसङ्कुलः ।
स्वकाले सत्यवद्भाति प्रबोधे सत्यसद्भवेत् ॥ ६ ॥

तावत्सत्यं जगद्भाति शुक्तिका रजतं यथा ।
यावन्न ज्ञायते ब्रह्म सर्वाधिष्ठानमद्वयम् ॥ ७ ॥

सच्चिदात्मन्यनुस्यूते नित्ये विष्णौ प्रकल्पिताः ।
व्यक्तयो विविधाः सर्वा हाटके कटकादिवत् ॥८॥

यथाकाशो हृषीकेशो नानोपाधिगतो विभुः ।
तद्भेदाद्भिन्नवद्भाति तन्नाशे केवलो भवेत् ॥९॥

नानोपाधिवशादेव जातिवर्णाश्रमादयः ।
आत्मन्यारोपितास्तोये रसवर्णादि भेदवत् ॥१०॥

पञ्चीकृतमहाभूतसम्भवं कर्मसञ्चितम् ।
शरीरं सुखदुःखानां भोगायतनमुच्यते ॥११॥

पञ्चप्राणमनोबुद्धिदशेन्द्रियसमन्वितम् ।
अपञ्चीकृतभूतोत्थं सूक्ष्माङ्गं भोगसाधनम् ॥१२॥

अनाद्यविद्यानिर्वाच्या कारणोपाधिरुच्यते ।
उपाधित्रितयादन्यम् आत्मानमवधारयेत् ॥१३॥

पञ्चकोशादियोगेन तत्तन्मय इव स्थितः ।
शुद्धात्मा नीलवस्त्रादियोगेन स्फटिको यथा ॥१४॥

वपुस्तुषादिभिः कोशैर्युक्तं युक्त्यवघाततः ।
आत्मानमन्तरं शुद्धं विविच्यात्तण्डुलं यथा ॥१५॥

सदा सर्वगतोऽप्यात्मा न सर्वत्रावभासते ।
बुद्धावेवावभासेत स्वच्छेषु प्रतिबिम्बवत् ॥ १६ ॥

देहेन्द्रियमनोबुद्धिप्रकृतिभ्यो विलक्षणम् ।
तद्वृत्तिसाक्षिणं विद्याद् आत्मानं राजवत्सदा ॥ १७ ॥

व्यापृतेष्विन्द्रियेष्वात्मा व्यापारीवाविवेकिनाम् ।
दृश्यतेऽभ्रेषु धावत्सु धावन्निव यथा शशी ॥ १८ ॥

आत्मचैतन्यमाश्रित्य देहेन्द्रियमनोधियः ।
स्वक्रियार्थेषु वर्तन्ते सूर्यालोकं यथा जनाः ॥ १९ ॥

देहेन्द्रियगुणान् कर्माण्यमले सच्चिदात्मनि ।
अध्यस्यन्त्यविवेकेन गगने नीलतादिवत् ॥ २० ॥

अज्ञानान्मानसोपाधेः कर्तृत्वादीनि चात्मनि ।
कल्प्यन्तेऽम्बुगते चन्द्रे चलनादि यथाम्भसः ॥ २१ ॥

रागेच्छासुखदुःखादि बुद्धौ सत्यां प्रवर्तते ।
सुषुप्तौ नास्ति तन्नाशे तस्माद्बुद्धेस्तु नात्मनः ॥ २२ ॥

प्रकाशोऽर्कस्य तोयस्य शैत्यमग्नेर्यथोष्णता ।
स्वभावः सच्चिदानन्दनित्यनिर्मलतात्मनः ॥ २३ ॥

109

आत्मनः सच्चिदंशश्च बुद्धेर्वृत्तिरिति द्वयम् ।
संयोज्य चाविवेकेन जानामीति प्रवर्तते ॥ २४ ॥

आत्मनो विक्रिया नास्ति बुद्धेर्बोधो न जात्विति ।
जीवः सर्वमलं ज्ञात्वा ज्ञाता द्रष्टेति मुह्यति ॥ २५ ॥

रज्जुसर्पवदात्मानं जीवं ज्ञात्वा भयं वहेत् ।
नाहं जीवः परात्मेति ज्ञातश्चेन्निर्भयो भवेत् ॥ २६ ॥

आत्मावभासयत्येको बुद्ध्यादीनीन्द्रियाण्यपि ।
दीपो घटादिवत्स्वात्मा जडैस्तैर्नावभास्यते ॥ २७ ॥

स्वबोधे नान्यबोधेच्छा बोधरूपतयात्मनः ।
न दीपस्यान्यदीपेच्छा यथा स्वात्मप्रकाशने ॥ २८ ॥

निषिध्य निखिलोपाधीन्नेति नेतीति वाक्यतः ।
विद्यादैक्यं महावाक्यैर्जीवात्मपरमात्मनोः ॥ २९ ॥

आविद्यकं शरीरादि दृश्यं बुद्बुदवत्क्षरम् ।
एतद्विलक्षणं विद्यादहं ब्रह्मेति निर्मलम् ॥ ३० ॥

देहान्यत्वान्नमे जन्मजराकार्श्यलयादयः ।
शब्दादिविषयैः सङ्गो निरिन्द्रियतया न च ॥ ३१ ॥

अमनस्त्वान्न मे दुःखरागद्वेषभयादयः ।
अप्राणो ह्यमनाः शुभ्र इत्यादि श्रुतिशासनात् ॥ ३२ ॥

एतस्माज्जायते प्राणो मनः सर्वेन्द्रियाणि च ।
खं वायुज्र्योतिरापः पृथिवी विश्वस्य धारिणी ॥ ३३ ॥

निर्गुणो निष्क्रियो नित्यो निर्विकल्पो निरञ्जनः ।
निर्विकारो निराकारो नित्यमुक्तोऽस्मि निर्मलः ॥ ३४ ॥

अहमाकाशवत्सर्वं बहिरन्तर्गतोऽच्युतः ।
सदा सर्वसमः सुद्धो निस्सङ्गो निर्मलोऽचलः ॥ ३५ ॥

नित्यशुद्धविमुक्तैकम् अखण्डानन्दमद्वयम् ।
सत्यं ज्ञानमनन्तं यत् परं ब्रह्माहमेव तत् ॥ ३६ ॥

एवं निरन्तराभ्यास ब्रह्मैवास्मीति वासना ।
हरत्यविद्याविक्षेपान् रोगानिव रसायनम् ॥ ३७ ॥

विविक्तदेशे आसीनो विरागो विजितेन्द्रियः ।
भावयेदेकमात्मानं तमनन्तमनन्यधीः ॥ ३८ ॥

आत्मन्येवाखिलं दृश्यं प्रविलाप्य धिया सुधीः ।
भावयेदेकमात्मानं निर्मलाकाशवत्सदा ॥ ३९ ॥

रूपवर्णादिकं सर्वं विहाय परमार्थवित् ।
परिपूर्णचिदानन्दस्वरूपेणावतिष्ठते ॥ ४० ॥

ज्ञातृज्ञानज्ञेयभेदः परे नात्मनि विद्यते ।
चिदानन्दैकरूपत्वाद् दीप्यते स्वयमेव तत् ॥ ४१ ॥

एवमात्मारणौ ध्यानमथने सततं कृते ।
उदितावगतिज्वाला सर्वाज्ञानेन्यनं दहेत् ॥ ४२ ॥

अरुणेनेव बोधेन पूर्वं सन्तमसे हृते ।
तत आविर्भवेदात्मा स्वयमेवांशुमानिव ॥ ४३ ॥

आत्मा तु सततं प्राप्तोऽप्यप्राप्तवदविद्यया ।
तन्नाशे प्राप्तवद्भाति स्वकण्ठाभरणं यथा ॥ ४४ ॥

स्थाणौ पुरुषवद् भ्रान्त्या कृता ब्रह्मणि जीवता ।
जीवस्य तात्त्विके रूपे तस्मिन्दृष्टे निवर्तते ॥ ४५ ॥

तत्त्वस्वरूपानुभवाद् उत्पन्नं ज्ञानमञ्जसा ।
अहं ममेति चाज्ञानं बाधते दिग्भ्रमादिवत् ॥ ४६ ॥

सम्यग्विज्ञानवान् योगी स्वात्मन्येवाखिलं जगत् ।
एकं च सर्वमात्मानम् ईक्षते ज्ञानचक्षुषा ॥ ४७ ॥

आत्मैवेदं जगत्सर्वम् आत्मनोऽन्यन्न विद्यते ।
मृदो यद्वद्घटादीनि स्वात्मानं सर्वमीक्षते ॥४८॥

जीवन्मुक्तस्तु तद्विद्वान् पूर्वोपाधिगुणांस्त्यजेत् ।
सच्चिदानन्दरूपत्वाद् भवेद्भ्रमरकीटवत् ॥४९॥

तीर्त्वा मोहार्णवं हत्वा रागद्वेषादिराक्षसान् ।
योगी शान्तिसमायुक्त आत्मारामो विराजते ॥५०॥

बाह्यानित्यसुखासक्तिं हित्वात्मसुखनिर्वृतः ।
घटस्थदीपवत्स्वस्थः स्वान्तरेव प्रकाशते ॥५१॥

उपाधिस्थोऽपि तद्धर्मैरलिप्तो व्योमवन्मुनिः ।
सर्वविन्मूढवत्तिष्ठेद् असक्तो वायुवच्चरेत् ॥५२॥

उपाधिविलयाद्विष्णौ निर्विशेषं विशेन्मुनिः ।
जले जलं वियद्व्योम्नि तेजस्तेजसि वा यथा ॥५३॥

यल्लाभान्नापरो लाभो यत्सुखान्नापरं सुखम् ।
यज्ज्ञानान्नापरं ज्ञानं तद्ब्रह्मेत्यवधारयेत् ॥५४॥

यद्दृष्ट्वा नापरं दृश्यं यद्भूत्वा न पुनर्भवः ।
यज्ज्ञात्वा नापरं ज्ञेयं तद्ब्रह्मेत्यवधारयेत् ॥५५॥

तिर्यगूर्ध्वमधः पूर्णं सच्चिदानन्दमद्वयम् ।
अनन्तं नित्यमेकं यत् तद्ब्रह्मेत्यवधारयेत् ॥५६॥

अतद्व्यावृत्तिरूपेण वेदान्तैर्लक्ष्यतेऽद्वयम् ।
अखण्डानन्दमेकं यत् तद्ब्रह्मेत्यवधारयेत् ॥५७॥

अखण्डानन्दरूपस्य तस्यानन्दलवाश्रिताः ।
ब्रह्माद्यास्तारतम्येन भवन्त्यानन्दिनोऽखिलाः ॥५८॥

तद्युक्तमखिलं वस्तु व्यवहारस्तदन्वितः ।
तस्मात्सर्वगतं ब्रह्म क्षीरे सर्पिरिवाखिले ॥५९॥

अनण्वस्थूलमह्रस्वम् अदीर्घमजमव्ययम् ।
अरूपगुणवर्णाख्यं तद्ब्रह्मेत्यवधारयेत् ॥६०॥

यद्भासा भास्यतेऽर्कादि भास्यैर्यत्तु न भास्यते ।
येन सर्वमिदं भाति तद्ब्रह्मेत्यवधारयेत् ॥६१॥

स्वयमन्तर्बहिर्व्याप्य भासयन्नखिलं जगत् ।
ब्रह्म प्रकाशते वह्निप्रतप्तायसपिण्डवत् ॥६२॥

जगद्विलक्षणं ब्रह्म ब्रह्मणोऽन्यन्न किञ्चन ।
ब्रह्मान्यद्भाति चेन्मिथ्या यथा मरुमरीचिका ॥६३॥

दृश्यते श्रूयते यद्यद् ब्रह्मणोऽन्यन्न तद्भवेत् ।
तत्त्वज्ञानाच्च तद्ब्रह्म सच्चिदानन्दमद्वयम् ॥ ६४ ॥

सर्वगं सच्चिदानन्दं ज्ञानचक्षुर्निरीक्षते ।
अज्ञानचक्षुर्नेक्षेत भास्वन्तं भानुमन्धवत् ॥ ६५ ॥

श्रवणादिभिरुद्दीप्तज्ञानाग्निपरितापितः ।
जीवः सर्वमलान्मुक्तः स्वर्णवद्द्योतते स्वयम् ॥ ६६ ॥

हृदाकाशोदितो ह्यात्मा बोधभानुस्तमोऽपहृत् ।
सर्वव्यापी सर्वधारी भाति भासयतेऽखिलम् ॥ ६७ ॥

दिग्देशकालाद्यनपेक्ष्य सर्वगं शीतादिहृन्नित्यसुखं निरञ्जनम् ।
यस्स्वात्मतीर्थं भजते विनिष्क्रियः स सर्ववित्सर्वगतोऽमृतो भवेत् ॥ ६८ ॥

॥ इति श्रीशङ्कराचार्यविरचित आत्मबोधः सम्पूर्णः ॥

ATMA BODHA

For the seeker made pure
  by the fire of devotion,
  for the seeker whose desires
  have been burnt to ash,
  for the seeker
  who shines with tranquility,
  for such a seeker
  no longer distracted,
  whose only prayer is to be free,
  is this *Atma Bodha* composed.   1

There is certainly
  no other way to know
  than through direct experience
  what is beyond the realm of the senses,
  what is beyond mind, intellect, or intuition.
Fire cooks food;
  there is no more
  immediate cause.
So, awaken.
Realize the inner light,
  and know the *atman* in all.   2

Goodness is not incompatible with binding action,
  does not cause delusions of mind to cease,
  does not halt the play of wisdom and ignorance.
Goodness is of the world
  and a sibling to gloom.   3

Concepts of self are limiting. Only
    primordial light destroys illusion.
Light shines forth from within,
    as if clouds had passed from the sun's face.   4

The soul, sullied by ignorance,
    becomes pure
    through study and practice.
What is learned then disappears,
    like the powder of the *kataka* nut
    that clears muddy water.   5

Wandering lost in the world of body and mind
    is like living in a dream.
Desire and aversion are twins;
    when either rules, the seeker sleepwalks.
The light of truth awakens.   6

The glint of an abalone shell
    may be mistaken for silver;
    so the world of the senses
    seems to shine.
Entranced, a seeker knows no
    unalloyed experience, though all of this
    world rests in the primordial.   7

The Lord[1] supports all.
The Lord is like the pure gold
    from which alloyed ornaments are created.
Created being is an expression
    of conscious brilliance.   8

Space fills pots of different shape and size.
So, the Lord dwells within all created form.
Let limitations be shattered,
   and know yourself to be whole.   9

Created being is myriad,
   though the *atman* is one in all.
Juice lends color and flavor to water;
   so, race, religion, class,
   and other temporal qualities
   tinge the clarity of being.   10

This physical body of earth,
   water, fire, air, and space
   is an expression of elapsed action.
Today's pleasure and pain are fleeting
   shadows of the past.   11

Vigor, intellect, passion,
   and sense experience,
   compose the subtle body.
Discipline awakens one to clear light.   12

Ignorance of unexplainable beginning
   shapes body and mind.
Three limitations:
   physical, subtle, and causal
   are imprinted upon the *atman*.   13

The soul veiled by the five illusions:
   body, breath, emotion, wisdom, and bliss
   takes on their characteristics,
   just as a crystal might
   appear to be a sapphire,
   when placed against blue cloth.   14

Threshing rice separates grain from husk.
Let discernment do the threshing,
   that you may know the *atman* beyond
   the three limitations and the five veils—
   chaff.   15

The *atman* is all-pervasive, though not
   apparent to everyone, everywhere.
Clear consciousness reflects the *atman*,
   just as a clean mirror reflects form
   without distortion.   16

Many think the *atman* to be created
   body, mind, or even intellect.
This is confusion.
Realize the inner witness.
Like a king, the *atman* rules
   ever over creation.   17

Like the king's ministers,
  body and mind serve in the world.
The ruling *atman* abides in stillness.
When clouds scud across the sky,
  the moon appears to move;
  so, when body and mind are in motion,
  the *atman* seems to act.   18

Daily duties can be undertaken
  only by the light of the sun.
 So, all action is illumated by the *atman*.   19

Unaware of the *atman*, most live deluded,
  mistaking themselves for body and mind.
One might as well mistake the sky
  for a finite blue dome, though
  the sky is indeed infinite space.   20

Confused seekers lay claim to action.
One might as well see the reflection
  of moonlight in a river and imagine
  that the moon itself moves
  with the water's ripples.   21

Passionate longing brings both
  joy and sorrow;
  these feelings are of the mind.
Like a dream that disappears
  during deep sleep,
  joy and sorrow vanish
  with the rising light of the *atman*.   22

One knows the sun by its light
   just as one knows water's cooling
   and fire's burning.
So, a seeker knows the *atman*
   as presence, awareness, and ecstasy—
   the ever-stainless primordial light.   23

I know. I need. I feel.
Thus says the mind mired in duality—
   so unfulfilled when not
   absorbed in the *atman*.
The mind's confusion brings about
   birth after birth.   24

Mind is ever in flux;
   yet mind can only express itself
   by the light of the *atman*,
   which knows no change.
How then does anyone live
   in slavish ignorance
   to the fluctuations of mind?   25

A seeker who mistakes
   a rope in the dark for a snake
   is frightened.
Likewise, one who confuses
   identity with body and mind
   is burdened by dread.
Realize the *atman*,
   and become fearless.   26

Planets do not illuminate the sun,
  nor do body and mind
  cast light upon the *atman*.
The light of the *atman* is like a flame
  shining through the openings of a lantern.   27

One who knows the *atman*
  desires nothing.
A lamp, once lit,
  is self-illuminating.   28

Do not let false notions bind you.
  Not this. Not this.
The great sayings reveal truth:
  I am Brahman.
  You are That.
  This atman is Brahman.
  Brahman is sheer ecstasy.   29

Identity is a product of ignorance.
This body and mind are like bubbles;
  how easy it is to be free
  of what is ephemeral.
Know only this: I am Brahman,
  effulgent and stainless.   30

I exist beyond creation.
I live free of body and mind.
I remain unaffected
  by birth, aging, illness, or death.
These are of the body, which I am not.
Neither do the senses
  bring me sorrow or joy.   31

I am unmoved by sorrow or joy,
   aversion or desire.
I know neither anger nor fear,
   nor could I cling to another,
     for all is in me, and I am in all.
I shine.   32

Breath, mind, and sense experience
   arise from the *atman*.
So, too, come forth the elements:
   space, wind, fire, water, and earth.
The *atman* births the universe,
   even as it conquers
     the seeker's infatuation with creation.   33

I am not limited by the science
   of the natural world.
I am timeless, simple, changeless,
   beyond form, and forever free.   34

I am like space.
I am everywhere,
   within and beyond,
   though I go nowhere.
I am the same in all—
   perfectly fulfilled,
   unattached,
   and so of steady connection.
I am forever resplendent.   35

Eternal, pure, and liberated,
  I am.
I am whole—
  an expression of truth[3] without parts.
I am ecstasy.
This *atman* is one with all.   36

Turn within, inquire steadily, and merge.
To merge with all is the elixir
  that heals the sickness of this world—
  the sorrows of a scattered mind
  and its afflictive habits.   37

One who longs to realize the *atman*
  must stoically conquer lust,
  find solitude, and sit.
Such boundless ecstasy
  is indivisible
  and knows no other.   38

Form dissolves into bliss.
One who seeks awakening
  merges with the *atman*
  and expands into space,
  undisturbed and limitless—
  eternal.   39

Stripping away ideas
  of beauty, class, or creed,
  one experiences sheer ecstasy—
  the full perfection of being.   40

The knower, the knowing,
  and what is to be known—
  all three are one, but
  to declare so asserts duality.
The *atman* is self-illuminating
  and makes no such distinctions.   41

Meditate on the *atman* alone
  to kindle the flame of truth.
This sacred fire burns desire to ash.
Action is sanctified.   42

The light of dawn rises
  red in the east
  and overcomes darkness.
When the light of the *atman* appears
  everywhere, delusion is dispelled.   43

Immature talk is silenced.
Awakening to the inner light
  is like suddenly remembering
  the resplendent necklace
  one has been wearing, all along.   44

The seeker might spot a tree
  in the dark and think it a man;
  so, the seeker whose mind wanders
  through the thicket of ignorance
  mistakes the self for body and mind.   45

At sunrise, a traveler realizes
  that during the night,
  the way was lost.
So, when knowledge dawns,
  concepts of I and mine
  are seen to be no more
  than the mind's digression.   46

The awakened one breathes
  throughout the universe.
One who sees with the eye of wisdom
  looks upon all of creation as the *atman*,
  for the *atman* is the very soul in all.   47

All manner of pots are shaped from clay.
So, each being is created of the *atman*,
  for there is none other than the *atman*.
One who looks deeply into another
  sees the self-same *atman*.   48

The cockroach kissed by a bee
  becomes itself a maker of honey.
So, one touched by light
  merges with that light,
  and sees through appearance.
The awakened one abandons
  sloth, passion, and even goodness
  for true existence.   49

The awakened one has crossed
  the sea of enchantment,
  slain the demons of duality.
So the sage is at peace,
  immersed in the brilliance
  of existence.   50

The awakened one loses interest
  in outer pleasure—
  unsatisfying.
The liberated sage shines
  like a lantern lit from within, lives
  absorbed in steady inner ecstasy.   51

The awakened one remains embodied.
Rooted in the mud of this world,
  yet undisturbed by the passions,
  the luminous sage blossoms.
As wind moves through the sky,
  so the awakened one walks the earth;
  the awakened one is like the sky.   52

Limitations disappear.
The sage is not constrained
  by body or mind,
  but completely lost in the Lord—
  as a river merges into ocean,
  wind into sky,
  and light into light.   53

That attained, there is nothing left
   to attain. There is no greater
   joy, and there is nothing
   more to know.
Such is realization of truth.   54

That seen, all is seen.
Having merged with the Lord,
   there is no return.
Such is realization of truth.   55

Above, below, and all around is pure
   existence, awareness, and bliss.
Ecstasy is indivisible,
   steady.
Such is realization of truth.   56

Flesh and thought are not truth.
Not this. Not this.
One who knows truth
   intimately
   knows no separation or craving,
   lives immersed in delight—
   endless ecstasy.
Such is realization of truth.   57

Ecstasy transcends form.
Even the savior is a small
   and fleeting
   expression of truth.   58

Be one with truth,
  and be whole, infinite.
Truth pervades interaction
  and yet transcends action.
As butter is in milk,
  so truth is latent within all.   59

Not subtle or solid,
  short or long,
  unborn or imperishable,
  formless or of nature.
Such is realization of truth.   60

Sun and moon do not illuminate
  truth, though they are themselves
  lit by the splendor of that primordial
  light by which all light shines.
Such is realization of truth.   61

Within, beyond, and throughout all
  shines truth.
Truth is self-luminous
  and lights the universe.
One who offers this life to truth,
  is radiant,
  like a metal orb glowing
  in the heat of a fire.   62

Truth is the source of creation,
  and truth abides as creation.
If anything is seen to be
  other than light,
  what misperception that is—
  a vision unreal as a mirage
  glimpsed in the desert.   63

Whatever is seen, heard,
  or sensed in any way
  is none other than truth.
Awareness of truth
  is the same as truth.
Truth is one
  with existence,
  consciousness,
  and bliss.   64

Though truth is everywhere,
  the ignorant perceive no truth.
After all, one who is blind
  does not see the sun's radiance.   65

Hearing of truth
  and contemplating truth,
  light wisdom's candle.
The seeker is purified
  like gold, releasing dross into fire.   66

The seeker awakens
  to the space of the heart.
Wisdom dispels ignorance,
  as light does darkness.
Splendor pervades all,
  supports all,
  and simply shines.   67

Truth is primordial—
  luminous throughout space and time,
  without cause.
The heart is the abode of boundless joy.
One who strives to realize the *atman*
  worships
  yet transcends ritual.
So, one awakens,
  free of all constraints,
  beyond even the bounds of death,
  to live ever omniscient and everywhere.   68

Such is the complete teaching of Atma Bodha
composed by Sri Sankaracarya.

NOTES

[1]Visnu.

[2]The "I" refers not to the personal self, but to the soul in union
with Brahman, or to that Brahman which is both immanent and
transcendent.

[3]Brahman.

DAILY PRAYERS

ॐ असतो मा सद्गमय ।
तमसो मा ज्योतिर्गमय ।
मृत्योर्मा अमृतं गमय ॥
ॐ शान्तिः शान्तिः शान्तिः ॥

ॐ लोकाः समस्ताः सुखिनो भवंतु ॥
ॐ शान्तिः शान्तिः शान्तिः ॥

ॐ पूर्णमदः पूर्णमिदं पूर्नात् पूर्नमुदच्यते ।
पूर्णस्य पूर्णमादाय पूर्णमेवावशिष्यते ॥
ॐ शान्तिः शान्तिः शान्तिः ॥

ॐ श्री गुरुभ्यो नमः हरिः ॐ ॥

Lead us from delusion to the truth.
Lead us from darkness to the light.
Lead us from the fear of death
to the blessings of immortal bliss.

May the whole world be joyful and free.

All of this creation is perfect.
Transcendent truth is perfect.
From absolute perfection arises
    what is perfect.
When we give to or receive from
    what is perfect,
that perfection remains perfect.
                    —*Isha Upanishad, Shantih Mantra*

I bow to every blessed teacher.

Om. Peace. Peace. Peace.

These mantras are prayers for liberation.

ॐ सर्वेशां स्वस्तिर्भवतु ।
सर्वेशां शान्तिर्भवतु ।
सर्वेशां पूर्णं भवतु ।
सर्वेशां मङ्गलं भवतु ॥
ॐ शान्तिः शान्तिः शान्तिः ॥

ॐ सर्वे भवन्तु सुखिनः
सर्वे सन्तु निरामयाः ।
सर्वे भद्राणि पश्यन्तु
मा कश्चिद्दुःख भाग्भवेत् ॥
ॐ शान्तिः शान्तिः शान्तिः ॥

May health be in all.
May joy be in all.
May fullness be in all.
May all be blessed.

May all be joyful.
May all enjoy good health.
May all see what is blessed.
May no one sorrow or suffer.

These mantras are chanted for good health and peace.

ब्रह्मार्पणं ब्रह्म हविर्ब्रह्माग्नौ ब्रह्मनाहुतम् ।
ब्रह्मैव तेन गन्तव्यं ब्रह्म कर्म समाधिना ॥

अन्नपूर्णे सदापूर्णे शङ्करप्रानवल्लभे ।
ज्ञानवैराग्यसिध्द्यर्थं भिक्षां देहि च पार्वति ॥

The act of sacrifice is the Lord.
The oblation itself is the Lord.
The Lord makes the offering to
the Lord, the sacred fire (within).
The Lord is to be realized
through such acts of sacrifice.

—Bhagavad Gita IV. 24

I bow to Mother Annapurna,
ever plentiful and benevolent.
You are the beloved of Lord Siva (Sankara).
Perfect us in freedom from illusory desires.
Bless us with this food of wisdom.

—Annupurna Stotram 11

These mantras are chanted to bless food before a meal is eaten.

ॐ शं नो मित्रः शं वरुणः ।

शं नो भवत्वर्यमा ।

शं नो इन्द्रो बृहस्पतिः ।

शं नो विष्णुरुरुक्रमः ।

नमो ब्रह्मणे ।

नमस्ते वायो ।

त्वमेव प्रत्यक्षं ब्रह्मासि ।

त्वमेव प्रत्यक्षं ब्रह्म वदिष्यामि ।

ऋतं वदिष्यामि ।

सत्यं वदिष्यामि ।

तन्मामवतु ।

तद्वक्तारमवतु ।

अवतु माम् ।

अवतु वक्तारं ।

ॐ शान्तिः शान्तिः शान्तिः ॥

May Mitra bless us. May Varuna bless us.
May the blessings of Aryama be upon us.
So with the blessings of Indra and Brhaspati.
May the all-pervasive Vishnu bless us.

I bow to the absolute Brahman.
I bow to you, Vayu.
You are the breath of the absolute,
made manifest.
I will proclaim the absolute.
I will speak the truth.
I will proclaim the absolute truth.

May that protect me.
May that protect the one who speaks.
Please guide me.
May you speak through me.
Peace. Peace. Peace.
—*Taittiriya Upanishad, Shantih Mantra*

*This mantra is chanted before lighting the lamp
and begining a class.*

ॐ सह नाववतु ।

सह नौ भुनक्तु ।

सह वीर्यं करवावहै ।

तेजस्वि नावधीतमस्तु ।

मा विद्विषावहै ॥

ॐ शान्तिः शान्तिः शान्तिः ॥

May the Lord protect us both.
May the Lord nourish us both.
May we accomplish our pursuit
with vigor and dignity. May our
studies be illuminating to all.
Om. Peace. Peace. Peace.

—Taittiriya Upanishad, Shantih Mantra

This mantra is chanted to bless studies.

ॐ भूर्भुव स्वः ।
तत् सवितुर्वरेण्यं ।
भर्गो देवस्य धीमहि ।
धियो यो नः प्रचोदयात् ॥
ॐ शान्तिः शान्तिः शान्तिः ॥

ॐ त्र्यम्बकं यजामहे ।
सुगन्धिं पुष्टिवर्धनम् ।
उर्वारुकमिव बन्धनान् ।
मृत्योर्मुक्षीय मामृतात् ॥
ॐ शान्तिः शान्तिः शान्तिः ॥

I bow to the earth, the heavens, and beyond,
to that radiance that illuminates all.
Let us meditate upon that light
that all may awaken to the truth of bliss.
                    —Rg Veda III.62.10

This mantra is chanted for the awakening of all beings.

We bow to the Lord of divine sight (three eyes),
the Lord who is full and sweet
and nourishes all life.
May we be liberated from bondage,
like a ripe melon from the vine,
and so realize the truth of immortal bliss.
                    —Rg Veda VII.59.12

This mantra is chanted for healing and liberation.

गुरुर्ब्रह्मा गुरुर्विष्णु र्गुरुर्देवो महेश्वरः ।
गुरुः साक्षात् परं ब्रह्मा तस्मै श्रीगुरवे नमः ॥

त्वमेव माता च पिता त्वमेव ।
त्वमेव बन्धुस्च सखा त्वमेव ।
त्वमेव विद्या द्रविणं त्वमेव ।
त्वमेव सर्वं मम देव देव ॥

कायेन वाचा मनसेन्द्रियैर्वा
बुध्यात्मना वा प्रकृतेः स्वभावात् ।
करोमि यद्यत् सकलं परस्मै
नारायणयेति समर्पयामि ॥

Brahma is the guru. Vishnu is the guru.
The great lord Siva is the guru.
The guru is before us.
The guru is beyond us.
I bow to the absolute guru, everywhere.
　　　　　　　　　—*Guru Gita 57*

You are my mother, my father, you are.
You are my true kin, my friend, you are.
You are my wisdom and wealth, you are.
You my all in all, light of all lights.
　　　　　　　　　—*Pandava Gita 28*

By body, speech, mind, or senses,
by intellect, soul, or entire being,
anything and all that I do for others,
I offer to the ever-present guru.
I surrender all to the absolute.
　　　　　　　　　—*Mukunda Mala 19*

समुद्र वसने देवि पर्वत स्तन मण्डले ।
विष्णु पत्नि नमस्तुभ्यं पाद स्पर्शं क्षमस्व मे ॥

ॐ अपवित्रः पवित्रो वा सर्वावस्थंगतोऽपि वा ।
यः स्मरेत्पुण्डरीकक्षं स बाह्याभ्यन्तरः शुचिः ॥

करचरण कृतं वाक्कायजं कर्मजं वा ।
श्रवणनयनजं वा मानसं वापराधं ।
विहितमविहितं वा सर्वमेतत्क्षमस्व ।
जय जय करुणाब्धो श्रीमहादेव शम्भो ॥

Mother Earth, adorned by the ocean and mountains,
beloved of Vishnu, I bow to you.
Forgive me for placing my feet upon you.

*This mantra is chanted before setting foot upon the earth
in the morning.*

Whether one is pure, impure,
under any circumstances,
upon remembering the lotus eyes of the Beloved,
all is purified, within and without.

*This mantra is for purification and may be chanted while
bathing.*

Whatever errors I have committed
with hands and feet, speech or body,
through my works,
by what I have seen or heard,
or in my thoughts,
while trying to attend to duties,
please forgive these.
Victory to you, Ocean of Compassion,
blessed Beloved Lord Siva.

*This prayer for forgiveness is often chanted in the evening
before going to bed.*

ॐ गजाननं भूतगणादि सेवितं
कपित्थ जम्बूफलसार भक्षितम् ।
उमासुतं शोक विनाशकारणं
नमामि विघ्नेश्वर पादपङ्कजम् ॥

I bow to the one of elephant face,
served by beings of light and earth,
who eats the essence of all fruit.
Son of the Divine Mother, you destroy
the cause of our sorrows.
I bow at your mud-born feet.

This mantra is chanted when entering a temple.

ॐ द्यौः शान्तिरन्तरिक्षं शान्तिः ।

पृथिवी शान्तिरापः शान्तिरोषधयः शान्तिः ।

वनस्पतयः शान्तिर्विश्वे देवाः शान्तिर्ब्रह्म शान्तिः ।

सर्वं शान्तिः शान्तिरेव शान्तिः सा मा शान्तिरेधि ॥

ॐ शान्तिः शान्तिः शान्तिः ॥

May peace be in the sky and vast space everywhere.
May peace be upon this earth,
in the water, trees, grass,and flowers.
May peace pervade the whole universe.
May divine peace dwell in the heart of all.
May there always be in all peace and only peace.
Peace. Peace. Peace.

—*Yajur Veda 36:17*

This mantra is chanted for peace, everywhere.

www.ingramcontent.com/pod-product-compliance
Lightning Source LLC
Chambersburg PA
CBHW032002040426
42448CB00006B/453